magic

words

 @**WORK**

Also by Howard Kaminsky and Alexandra Penney

Magic Words

Also by Howard Kaminsky,
co-written with Susan Kaminsky

The Glow

The Seventh Child

Talent

The Twelve

The Storyteller

Also by Alexandra Penney

How to Make Love to a Man

How to Make Love to Each Other

Why Men Stray and Why Men Stay

How to Make Love to a Man (Safely)

BROADWAY BOOKS NEW YORK

magic
words
@WORK

powerful phrases

to help you conquer

the working world

HOWARD KAMINSKY and ALEXANDRA PENNEY

PRINTED IN THE UNITED STATES OF AMERICA

BROADWAY BOOKS and its logo, a letter B bisected on the diagonal, are trademarks of Random House, Inc.

Visit our website at www.broadwaybooks.com

First edition published 2004

Library of Congress Cataloging-in-Publication Data
Kaminsky, Howard.
    Magic words at work : powerful phrases to help you conquer the working world / Howard Kaminsky and Alexandra Penney.—1st ed.
        p.   cm.
    1. Success in business—Quotations, maxims, etc.   2. Life skills—Quotations, maxims, etc.   3. Self-help techniques.   I. Penney, Alexandra. II. Title.

HF5386.K1545 2004
650.1—dc22

                                                                2003057751

ISBN 0-7679-1441-4

10   9   8   7   6   5   4   3   2   1

For our magical friends

Paige and Ken

Melinda and Ealan

And for Susan Dooley Carey, the alchemist

acknowledgments

Grateful thanks to our editor, Kris Puopolo, whose wizardry guided us every step of the way. And to Steve Rubin, who was the first to see the magic. And to Susan, Dennis, Jessica, Dave, John, Julie, and little Celeste, who give us some of their magic every day.

contents

MANAGING SHOULDER

TO SHOULDER

MANAGING UP

MANAGING DOWN

preface

Business loves buzz words. From Norman Vincent Peale's "Power of Positive Thinking" to the recent "Thinking Outside the Box," catchphrases give us new ways to view the world we work in. Some are particular to a profession, like the order issued in universities to "Publish or perish," or the one journalists hate hearing from editors, "Beef it up and boil it down," a harsh directive to make the story meatier in content and nowhere near as long. But the problem with these phrases, whether they are general or particular, is that they quickly grow stale. Familiar to everyone, they are devoid of any personal meaning.

Our first book, *Magic Words—101 Ways to Talk Your Way Through Life's Challenges,* was the result of our collecting essential and powerful catchwords and mantras we used ourselves and had heard over the years from friends and colleagues. So we weren't surprised when the response to that volume of Magic Words included many letters telling us how our readers had evolved their own specific phrases to help them in their jobs. Or, as one person put it, "I guess you could call them Magic Words for making money." We heard this from so many people that we decided to put together another volume—*Magic Words at Work.*

This book is divided into four sections: Managing Yourself, because until you understand and motivate this employee the game can't start; Managing Shoulder to Shoulder, which will help you focus on working and succeeding with others; Managing Up, to enable you to understand and deal with *the* crucial person, Mr. or Ms. Boss; and Managing Down, which provides you with time-tested Magic Words to help with the truly key people—your employees.

A man who owns a small business wrote us that he has a sign reading "Low Overhead Equals High Independence" to remind him not to take on the kind of debt that could crush his company. A woman who grew up poor says when her job gets rough she focuses on all the things she can afford to buy. She says she truly believes, "The person who dies with the most toys wins."

And in case you are wondering why the two of us felt that our careers stood in need of Magic Words, it's because between us we've experienced almost every situation we've written about in this book. We have tired of one career and moved on to another, held high positions in some companies and worked for others where takeovers or mergers wiped out our jobs. We have successfully marketed our own ideas, hired people and fired them, found there were flaws in the way we managed some things and discovered useful tricks that helped us to handle others. In the more than twenty years we've been friends, each of us has helped the other through the satisfactions and disappointments that come with any career. We've always been there for each other, handing out kudos, compassion—and occasionally kicks.

One reason our friendship has endured is our shared belief in the power of Magic Words. For two decades they have been a verbal kaleidoscope for us—a twist of phrase here, a turn there, and suddenly we begin to see things in a completely new way. Once, when we were having lunch, Alexandra complained that she was having trouble getting the head of the company to listen to her ideas. Howard, knowing that Alexandra felt hesitant about putting herself forward in a new job, told her, "Raising your voice can work better than raising your hand." For a moment, Alexandra sat there in silent astonishment. Was Howard really suggesting that shouting and hitting people were useful tools for getting attention? Then, in a single click of the kaleidoscope, she understood. She had let her timidity in a new job destroy her confidence. Howard's Magic Words were telling her that she was raising a hand, waiting to be called on, instead of being sure of what she had to say and raising her voice so people could hear her say it.

Some of the Magic Words at Work are useful guides to dealing with employees. "Above Me Is No-Man's-Land" is a way of warning staff members not to go over your head when problems arise. The words may sound like a threat, but they're more than that. They let the people who work for you know that a company has an organization chart for a reason. The place where a problem originates is the place where it should be solved.

One friend told us how his discovery of the Magic Words "The Red Light Is On" gave him time to deal with his own work problems without interruptions from his staff. "Ready, Aim, Fire" is another's mantra, and it lays out the course he follows when he has to tell employees that they're out of a job.

Other Magic Words are about the way we deal with our own careers. "Martyrs Are Revered (but Rarely Rewarded)" convinced someone else that there's a difference between working hard and working smart. The words "Graduate with Honors" are a warning that we never really leave a job behind; hard as this may be, it pays to exit smiling. Old employers have the power to send out letters that recommend us or to say that we failed on the job.

Lastly, there are Magic Words that tell us how to think about the world of work. " 'Good Enough' Isn't" is a quick way to remember that shortcuts won't get us anywhere; we should always do our best on the job. "The Trumpet Is a Dangerous Instrument"? Remember those words when you are about to sound your own horn. People who praise themselves will find that no one else will bother.

The last—and maybe the most important—thing we learned from our collection of Magic Words at Work is that work should be as satisfying as we can make it. When a close friend told us that the words that had guided her career were "You Mean It's Not Fun Anymore?" we didn't think she was being at all frivolous. Fun should be one of the many rewards that we get from our jobs. If you're failing to find it in yours, it may be that you need a little bit of magic to enhance your career.

MANAGING YOURSELF

ACHILLES WAS LUCKY

We've both known Sara for almost twenty years. Her creative ability and her strength as a manager have landed her a job as editor in chief of a top women's magazine, but back in the days when she was just starting out, Sara was a features editor at a small magazine. That's how Alexandra, who was working as a freelance writer, met her. She got a call from Sara, inviting her to lunch.

"I've got an assignment for you," Sara told her. "It's a little different from what you usually write."

"You've got my attention."

"Do you remember the *Iliad*?"

"I read it in college. I loved it."

"Do you recall Achilles' one weakness?"

"What is this? A quiz show?"

"Go along with me on this."

"Okay, teacher. It was his heel."

"You get an A. Now, Alexandra, do you think most people have a weakness? No, let's call it a flaw."

"That's easy. Of course they do."

"What would you say yours is?"

"That's easy, too. I'm terrible about returning phone calls. Except when it's to an editor, of course."

Sara looked approving, as though Alexandra had earned herself another A.

"You've just proved my theory, and I think it will make a great piece. Here's my idea. I've always believed that everyone has more than one flaw. We usually pick one that's fairly mild, acknowledge it, and ignore the others. Lucky Achilles. Can you imagine how nice it would be to have only one weakness? Take me, for example. Except for work, I'm always late. I know it. I admit it to friends, and I actually try to work on it. I've improved a bit, but in the meantime my husband has pointed out that, while I'm owning up to that flaw, I have another one which is actually worse. I have a terrible temper, and I lose it over small things. I mean, really tiny things. I pat myself on the back because I've been on time and then blow up because someone else has beaten me to a parking space. So, as my husband puts it, I have a sweet little flaw that I acknowledge, and a big bad flaw that I don't. How about it, Alexandra? Are you willing to interview people and get them to tell you the sweet little flaw and then prod them into pulling out the big bad one?"

Alexandra was, and it produced a great article. One chef initially confessed to an unwillingness to share his Chinese food when eating out with friends, and then, asked to try again, admitted that he really hated having women in his kitchen. There was the woman copywriter who coyly revealed an aversion to sharing taxicabs and then, pressed, admitted that she was so tightfisted that she recycled gifts she didn't want and gave them to her staff at Christmas.

So what is the point of these Magic Words? They're a reminder that if we're like most people, we've chosen to acknowledge a fairly harmless flaw and may be letting something far more serious get in the way of our success. Unlike Achilles, who knew the danger of his heel, we aren't always aware of the flaws that can do us harm. The chef who hated female kitchen staff had to acknowledge it to deal with it—certainly every woman who'd ever applied to him for a job had picked up on what he felt. And the copywriter's tightfisted giving was a common source of complaint in her office. Alexandra's long-ago article taught her that it pays to move past the innocent quirk—in herself and others—and look for the flaw that really causes problems.

CHEW, CHEW, CHEW

"Chew your food," our mothers used to say. And even though they didn't insist that we chew each mouthful a hundred times before swallowing, they made it clear that gulping things down was not only bad manners, it was also bad for the digestion.

"Momilies," as author Michele Slung has labeled those homilies handed down by generations of moms, can be the bane of our lives or, as in this instance, they can remind us that the things our mothers used to say may contain valuable lessons.

Recently, Beth, an old friend of Howard's, had dinner with us. We were celebrating her first day on a new job, a job she had lusted for, but one that, she now confessed, might be too much for her to handle.

Beth's area was market research, and her new job at a big advertising agency placed her right below the president—the number-two slot at the agency. Right after she walked into her office that morning—before she even had time to find the ladies' room or visit the company cafeteria—the head of the agency plopped a three-hundred-page report on her desk.

As Beth stared at the thick portfolio, Dave tapped it with his hand and said, "This is very important, Beth. I want you to read it carefully, not once but twice, and then see me."

"What is it?"

"It's a report I commissioned from a management-consulting firm on how to completely restructure our market-research department both here and overseas."

"I can't wait to read it," Beth said gamely.

"Good," Dave replied, "because that's just the start. I want you to be in charge of implementing the reorganization."

"All I could think of was the twelve labors of Hercules," Beth said to us, crumbling a piece of bread on the small plate. "Now I know how the poor guy felt when he was given the task of cleaning out the Augean stables. Reorganizing the entire agency! The task's immense. I'm new, I don't even know where to begin. Maybe I'm in over my head."

"This calls for the chew approach," said Alexandra, who signaled the waiter to bring another bottle of wine.

"What's that?" asked Beth.

"Maybe Howard should explain."

"I was always in a hurry as a kid," said Howard. "Nothing unusual there. Nor was it unusual that when I sat down to dinner I wasn't thinking of the food, I was thinking about finishing fast so that I could go outside and play ball with my friends. Naturally, my mother was always trying to slow me down: 'Chew your food!' One day she got so frustrated with the way she'd tell me to chew and all I'd do was gulp that she got up from the table, came over to me, and picked up my plate. I thought, 'Oh, great, now I can go out and play,' but she made me sit back down. She took my plate out to the kitchen and separated the food onto four salad plates. She put them in a line in front of me. 'One thing at a time, Howard. Chew!' It became a family joke," said Howard.

"Until you grew up," Alexandra interjected. "Eventually, Beth, Howard realized that it was good advice for a lot of things. Some projects are so big they're intimidating. Look at the whole picture and you'll freeze. So, whenever I get overwhelmed at the job, Howard always says, 'Chew, Chew, Chew.' It reminds me that you *can't* gulp things down. Things get done one bite at a time."

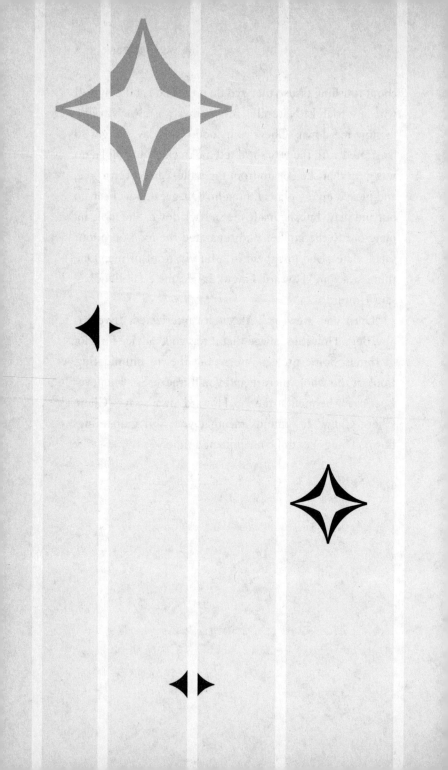

We've both worked with many successful executives, and almost all of them had one trait in common. Smart? Of course. Hardworking? Obviously. Tough when they have to be? Natch. But the trait we're talking about is the ability to be on time.

When Howard was just starting out in publishing, he met Ned at a booksellers' convention. Ned was only five years older than Howard, but everyone could see he was going to go far. He had taken a small, failing firm and within three years had turned it around, making it one of the major companies dealing in mass-market paperbacks.

Ned and Howard became good friends, and though Howard never worked for him, Ned taught him an important business lesson. Ned was always on time.

"Whether it was meeting Ned for a drink or having lunch or dinner with him, I never got there ahead of him," Howard says. "He'd always be sitting there, his favorite drink, a Kir Royale, sitting in front of him. One day I asked him two questions: How do you always manage to be early? And why does it matter to you?

"Being early is easy," Ned said. "I keep my watch set a half-hour fast. I've been doing it since college." Howard thought about that, and though he didn't say anything to Ned, he realized that idea wouldn't work for him. "It wouldn't be long before I'd begin to automatically subtract that half-hour. The way I'd see it, my watch was hoarding a little extra time for me, and pretty soon I'd start taking it."

So Howard moved on to "Why?"

"I like to be early because it allows me time to think of what I'd like to talk about. It's also nice to be able to sit here and enjoy my drink and think about how my day has gone.

"I've always called it 'Wrist Power,'" Ned continued. "Being on time is really using time well. Making it work for you. People who arrive late have the mistaken idea that they're making every minute count. They're not. People who show up late for meetings have already given me the edge. They start out apologizing, they're feeling harried because they meant to be just a little bit late and then a truck backed out of an alley and blocked their cab. So, instead of spending the time en route to the meeting thinking about what they want to say, they're thinking about the truck, or about the stoplight. Meanwhile, I'm here, enjoying a drink, thinking about what I want to accomplish in the meeting. I'm not scurrying around distracted by traffic and wondering how late I'm going to be. I'm already here."

Howard confesses that this point of view was new to

him. It was also one he found very persuasive. He had left the office at the last possible minute, been held up by the very truck Ned had mentioned, and arrived at the restaurant apologetic and frazzled. Those extra minutes he'd put in at the office had been far fewer than the ones he'd wasted fretting about the slow taxi ride.

"An important part of my dedication to 'Wrist Power' is also courtesy," Ned added. "People who are chronically late are discounting the value of your time. Or they want to be the center of attention, and it's easier to achieve that when they make a grand—and late—entrance. I start meetings on time and I end them that way. Unless my car blows up along the way, I'm at the airport early enough to sit and read the paper before boarding. There's enough stress that we can't avoid. I'm not perfect, far from it, but the one thing I know I can control is being on time."

Although neither of us set our watches ahead a half-hour, we both subscribe to "Wrist Power." Strategically, there *is* power in being there first, in being calm and prepared when the latecomer hurries in full of apologies for behavior that is every bit as rude as not saying "please" or "thank you." Effective managers may tolerate a flurry of lateness in someone else because they feel it gives them an advantage. Personally, they'll practice "Wrist Power," because lateness doesn't make you look important, it makes you look incompetent.

LET'S PRETEND

Howard and Alexandra came up with these Magic Words one afternoon after spying a mutual friend walking down the opposite side of the street. Marjorie had just gone back to work after a ten-year hiatus at home with her young family. When Howard and Alexandra spotted her striding up Madison Avenue, she was wearing a thigh-high skirt, chunky wedge-heeled shoes, and a tight short-sleeved sweater that rode up as she walked, exposing an inch or more of midriff.

"I thought you said that Marjorie had gotten a job with a law firm," said Howard, staring at Marjorie's outfit.

"She has," said Alexandra. "Want to bet she won't stay there long?"

Howard refused the bet, but Alexandra was unable to resist telling him why she'd been willing to put down ten dollars on the likelihood that Marjorie was in line for a new career.

"She's playing 'Let's Pretend,' " Alexandra explained. "I

think she already knows she doesn't want to work in that law office. She's dressing for the job she wishes she had, not for the one she's got. Here's my bet—contracts for a theatrical agent."

Alexandra was a little off. When Howard ran into Marjorie six months later, she was working as counsel for a large record company. The encounter with Marjorie got Howard and Alexandra thinking about how dress can affect your career. It also made Alexandra a proponent of what she calls the Cary Grant Approach, named for the actor who was a synonym for sophistication and who once confided, "I pretended to be somebody I wanted to be, and I finally became that person."

This was the tactic adopted by a young woman Alexandra knew who worked as a secretary for a fashion magazine. Deborah's dream was to be a fashion editor, and long before she had the job, she had the image. Because she was young, she wisely shunned the stark, sophisticated perfection of a Diana Vreeland, and instead, in her clothes and hairstyle, mirrored the fashion fads of people her age who were making news in the worlds of art, music, and drama. Deborah was never outlandish, but she was always different and completely original. Gradually, senior editors began seeking her advice on styles that were percolating up from the underground. One day, one of the editors asked that Deborah be made her assistant. There is no question in anyone's mind that Deborah will eventually take the step up to editor. To look at her, you'd think she was already there.

Howard saw the same thing happen with a young mail-room clerk at his publishing house. Shunning the casual clothes worn by other gofers, James wore tweeds and loafers and—Howard says this is what first caught his attention—carried a rolled-up copy of a small literary magazine in his jacket pocket. Because James's dress was unusual for his job, people noticed him and treated him differently from the other clerks. The protruding magazine started conversations, and James's earnest desire to have a role in the world of literature made several editors adopt him as a protégé. Although editorially James is on the bottom rung, dealing with the unsolicited manuscripts known as the slush pile, he got the part he dressed for. Howard says that if he shows up in scrubs everyone will know that James has decided to switch to medicine.

Dressing the part is what Alexandra calls "Let's Pretend." Sometimes it's a way of convincing other people you're right for the role. But sometimes it's a way of trying on a new profession. When a photographer we know was thinking of giving up the unsettled life of the freelancer for law school, a lawyer friend told her that first she should play "Let's Pretend." "Buy a silk blouse and a tailored suit and wear them for a week. If you can't stand the outfit," he warned her, "I promise you you'll hate the job."

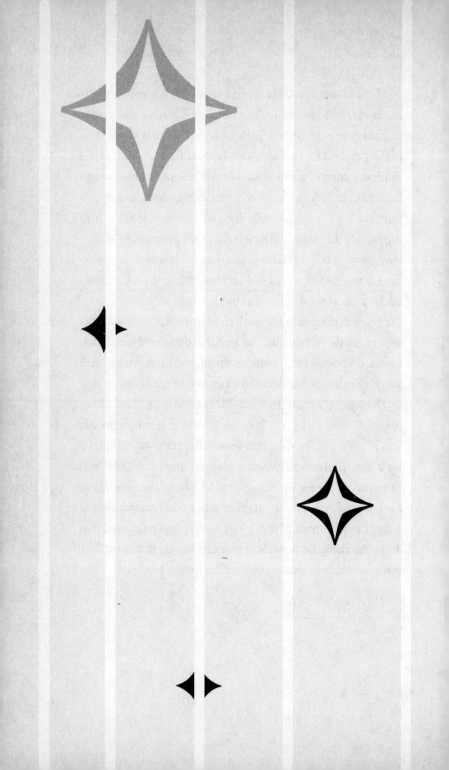

IN, OUT, AND THINK ABOUT

These Magic Words were given to Alexandra by Jody, who claims that the most efficient member of her staff is that old pro, "crastination." Jody, despite her affection for bad puns, is an extremely competent woman, an account executive at a large advertising agency. She even dresses efficiently, avoiding the fads and frills of fashion and invariably appearing with her dark hair drawn back into a simple ponytail, wearing one of her many tailored black suits and her trademark jewelry, a heavy gold chain-link necklace and gold link earrings. She and Alexandra were talking about one of Jody's clients, and Jody mentioned several other companies she planned to approach. "I'm finally beginning to think creatively," she announced, surprising Alexandra by admitting that, for her first three months as an account executive, she had felt overwhelmed by the day-to-day details of the job.

"I'm a neatnik," Jody said. "I function best when things are orderly, but I never seemed able to clear off my desk.

The clutter kept me from thinking. My secretary tried to help by making piles on the conference table, but that was worse. Out of reach, they seemed even more out of my control. Then I remembered that, when I was in grade school and took my first exam, my teacher told us all that we should answer the questions we knew and skip past the ones we weren't sure of. When we came to the end of the exam, she said, we could go back and work on the ones that needed more time. That way, we'd be sure to get some things right.

"It struck me that the problems piling up on my desk were like the questions in an exam. Some I could deal with immediately, some I needed to think about. I jokingly told my secretary that it wasn't enough to have an in box and an out box. I needed a box for things I wanted to think about. I came in on Monday morning and found that she'd taken me literally. Between the in box and the out, there was a third box, which said 'Think About.' That box has changed my life."

Jody was acknowledging what we often ignore: sometimes procrastination is a good idea. Instead of letting things pile up in her in box so that she feels as though she's always behind, Jody deals with the easy things first, moving them quickly from in to out, and postpones the difficult decisions by consigning them to the middle box. Once a week, Jody goes through "Think About." "You can't just forget the problems are there," she cautions. "Every week, when I go through the things I've put off dealing with, I find that half the problems have already solved themselves. On others, I have a better idea of what I want to see done. And there are always a few that get put back to ripen further. When people raise an eyebrow at that middle box, I quote the sixteenth-century physician Paracelsus: 'Anyone who imagines that all fruits ripen at the same time as the strawberries knows nothing about grapes.' The words have become a mantra for the office. At staff meetings, when anyone starts to complain about being overwhelmed, someone at the meeting chants, 'In, Out, and Think About.'"

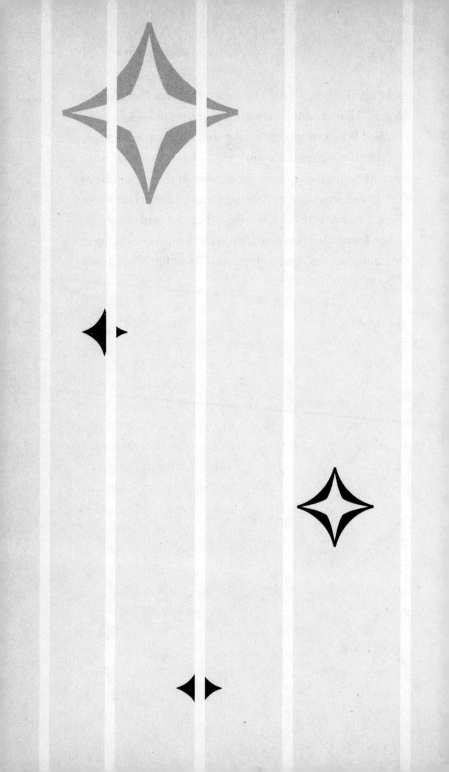

YOU CAN'T SELL HOTCAKES
WHEN THEY'RE COLD

These are Ellen's Magic Words. She learned the hard way that it is not good business to let too much time elapse between the idea and the execution. Though she has a degree in landscape architecture, Ellen discovered early in her career that the grand design had little meaning for her. She was, as they say in her trade, a dirt gardener, someone who is happiest puttering around with plants. When she married Tom, she gave up her job with a landscaping firm and took a job at a local horticultural center, propagating plants.

When Tom's company transferred them to another state, Ellen decided to start her own nursery. Her first summer was a success, but Ellen knew that her new business needed to generate income during the off-season. At the end of August, she sat down and planned a series of winter workshops, covering all aspects of horticulture, from plant propagation to healing with herbs.

Once she made up her schedule, Ellen set it aside and concentrated on the day-to-day chores that come with running a nursery. If you'd asked her why she hadn't gotten around to hiring the designer to produce the brochure, contacting the printer, and putting together a mailing list of her customers, she would have countered with the words her busy mother had used when her children had begged to be taken to the zoo: "A plan that's good today will be just as good tomorrow."

What may be true of trips to the zoo is not necessarily true of business. What tomorrow brought was a brochure from a rival nursery, offering winter courses almost identical to the ones Ellen had planned.

Ellen had convinced herself that her idea was unique, and that it was safely locked in her head, where no one else could take it. It never occurred to her that even "unique" scientific discoveries often occur simultaneously in several different places, and that many a teaching assistant dallying over a doctoral dissertation has found that someone else has published the theory first. When you have a great idea, it's best to assume that the same lightbulb has popped on in someone else's brain.

Wait too long and you risk not only that someone else will use your idea first, but also that the situation that inspired your brainstorm may change. Sometimes it takes only a month to turn an idea whose time has come into an idea whose time has gone. If you're going to manufacture thousands of T-shirts bearing the name of a Super Bowl contender, they have to hit the market before the team hits the skids.

In the world of ideas, Ellen's story is a minor one, but it taught us that inspiration is only as good as the action that follows it. And it gave us the Magic Words "You Can't Sell Hotcakes When They're Cold."

Lee called Alexandra to say that he was in town for two days. Could she have dinner? Lee, her computer guru back in the days when she'd despaired of ever learning the difference between a megabyte and a RAM, had long since given up guiding novices through the world of wizziegigs and now had a thriving computer company of his own in Massachusetts.

After they'd ordered, Alexandra studied Lee, a good-looking man in his thirties whose dark brush haircut makes him look younger than he is, and asked, "Are you happy with the company? Is it doing well?"

Lee grinned and said, "If you'd asked me that question two months ago, I would have said yes to the latter and no to the former. The company was doing too well, and I wasn't happy because I always felt under pressure. Everyone wanted a piece of my day, and I was working all night to get everything done. I was exhausted, and I was beginning to wonder if I wouldn't be better off shutting down and going to work for someone else. It took all my will-power not to get irritable when I had things I needed to do and people on the staff kept demanding my help."

"Can't your assistant say you're busy?" Alexandra asked.

"You mean the dragon at the gate? That's the old way. Hierarchical. Shutting people out," said Lee, one of many young entrepreneurs who have discovered that the new style of open-to-all management has problems, too.

"Could you take a course in management?" Alexandra asked. "They could teach you how to best use your time."

"That's exactly what I did," Lee said, grinning. "Only it wasn't taught by a university. It was taught by my six-year-old niece, Hannah."

Lee explained that he was so exhausted that he decided to take the weekend off to visit his brother in New Hampshire. His sister-in-law, a bit of a matchmaker, sent Lee on an errand to a woman who lives nearby.

With his niece as guide, Lee walked down the road to the woman's house. "Uh-oh!" Hannah said, as they approached the door. "We can't go in."

"Why not?" Lee asked.

"Look!" his niece pointed. "The red ribbon is on the knob."

His niece explained that she and her friends often visited the woman, a potter who would give them cookies and let them make small clay figures in her studio. "She said she wants us to come but sometimes she's busy. She told us she'd put a red ribbon on the door when we couldn't come in. Otherwise, we come whenever we want. That's the rule," Hannah said firmly. "Red means stop."

On the walk back, Lee remembered that when he was a youngster his grandfather had hung a red light over the door to his workshop. Lee and his brother were welcome to enter unless the light was on. Back in Boston, Lee didn't go straight to his office on Monday morning. He visited a hardware store.

"After a little fiddling with extension cords," Lee told Alexandra, "I called a staff meeting and explained that I wanted them all to feel free to come into my office anytime—except when the red light was on. That meant I had something urgent that I had to do, and that I needed some uninterrupted time. It's been a charm. No one gets their feelings hurt, because the red light excludes everyone. I have time to sort things out, get my priorities straight, and attend to what really needs doing. When I get to feeling pressured, I just start the morning by telling myself, 'The Red Light Is On.' "

Lee's words can work without the accompanying hardware. Whenever you need time for yourself—personally or professionally—just tell people, "The Red Light Is On." Oh, and by the way, one other good thing came of that weekend. Having reduced the pressure of work, Lee found time to return to his brother's house, make another trip down the road, and meet the potter. "I knew I'd like a woman who'd figured out how to take her own time without hurting anyone's feelings."

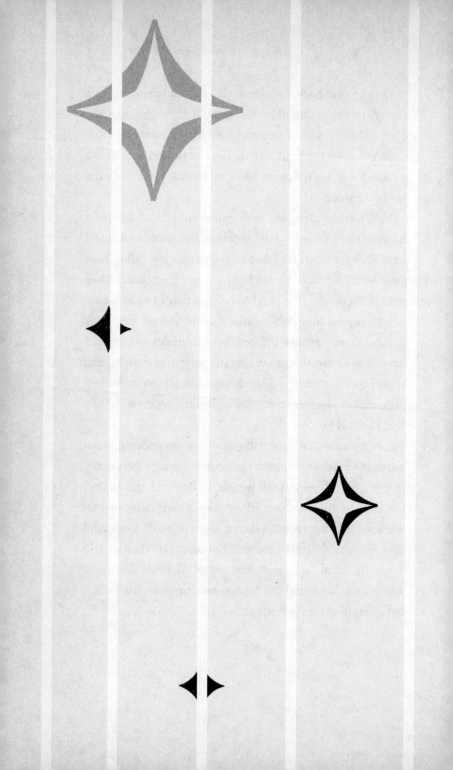

"GOOD ENOUGH" ISN'T

"My husband is a very impatient man," said Susannah, who lives an hour outside of Albany and runs an organization that provides counseling for troubled teenagers. She was explaining to Alexandra the origin of her Magic Words. "We have a small farm, and it's full of fence posts that don't stand straight, slapdash paint jobs, and gates that don't quite close. One weekend, shortly after we'd bought the place, we were fencing off a section of pasture and put up over a hundred feet of fence upside down. The small holes, which were supposed to be at the bottom to keep the chickens from getting out, were at the top. I pointed this out to Jack and, sighing, said we'd have to take it all down.

" 'No way we're doing it all over again,' he protested, dropping his hammer on the ground and walking back toward the house. 'It's good enough.'

"Obviously it wasn't, and after a brief quarrel we set the fence right side up. Over the years, Jack's tendency to declare a project done with the phrase 'Good enough' became a family joke. But it also became an insidious encouragement to settle for second best. I'd find myself rushed at work during the week, anxious to leave the city and get home to the farm, and I'd mutter, 'Good enough,' and finish off something that really should have been given more time.

"About a year ago, I did that with a funding proposal I was submitting. There was one section that was weak. It really needed more research than I'd given it. But that would have meant working late and probably staying overnight in the city. And that would have meant that I'd have to explain to Jack what our youngest needed for school and what was in the freezer for dinner. It all seemed too much, so I convinced myself that what I'd done was adequate, that the project rested on its own merits. All the things we tell ourselves when we don't want to go the extra step.

"We didn't get the funding, and even though no one else in the office blamed me, I knew it was my fault. I'd gone with 'Good Enough,' but 'Good Enough Isn't.' "

Susannah told Alexandra that her own Magic Words, which she uses to counter Jack's tendency to slough things off, have also had an effect on her children. "They were beginning to follow their father, assuming that you could get away with sloppy work. The more I counter with my own Magic Words, the more they begin to see that it's important to always do your very best, that 'Good Enough Isn't.' "

THE SCARLET SIGNS

We live in a world of signs. When you're in the car and see the sign SOFT SHOULDER, you immediately edge toward the middle of the road. The now ubiquitous sign NO SMOKING gives the tobacco-addicted the bad news that cigarette smoking isn't allowed. And everybody understands WARNING: THIN ICE, though some may be foolish enough to disregard it.

There are cautionary signs in the workplace as well, though they aren't written in capital letters and posted in plain sight. We do not wish to encourage paranoia, but there are times when a failure to recognize the warning signs can cost you your job.

Eleanor, who used to work for a government agency, says she learned that the new head of her division did not hold her in high esteem when she failed to receive copies of a brochure she'd edited. She called the printer to ask him to send them and he told her he couldn't: her name had been removed from the distribution list.

Eleanor didn't need a second warning that the change in management had put her job in jeopardy, and she immediately sent out feelers that eventually resulted in a new position. It is silly to see "Scarlet Signs" in what may merely be oversights, but if meetings you would once have attended are now being held without you—not just one meeting or two, but many—you're being pushed to the side. And once you've been sidelined, one more push can knock you out.

Memos, or your failure to receive them, are another "Scarlet Sign." Our friend Stephanie calls them the jungle drums of the office. When it comes to who gets told what, there are short, exclusive lists for really important information; there are medium-length lists to notify middle managers about changes in operation; there are what we call the y'all-come lists, which go to everyone and usually contain nothing more serious than notification of a holiday or an office collection for someone's farewell present. If you were once on the short list and suddenly find the only memos you're getting are asking for money to buy pregnant Patty a present, the jungle drums are sending you very bad news.

Travel authorization is also a sign, but one that can work both ways. Sometimes the warning comes when none of your travel plans are approved. A fashion reporter for a major urban newspaper got justifiably nervous when her editor vetoed her annual trip to Paris to view the spring collections. These were not budget cuts which were made across the board: the film critic was still sent off to Cannes.

On the other hand, an architect Howard knows was given a one-way ticket to Ontario, assigned to oversee the design and construction of a quite ordinary hotel. This put him out of the office for six months, in the middle of a time when he and the firm's other young architects had been vying for the right to design an innovative office building. If going is good and you're told to stay, that's bad; if going is bad and you're sent on your way, you've been given "The Scarlet Sign."

Delays are another indication that you're being squeezed out. Projects you've promoted are put on hold. The new chair you ordered for your assistant never shows up, and when you call Purchasing to complain, the agent says the boss never sent the requisition form. You're told that your request for a meeting with the vice-president will have to wait until he returns from Europe, and then, when he returns, that it will have to wait until he gets caught up.

If you've been goofing off on the job, "The Scarlet Sign" may be your last chance to improve your performance. But when there's been a change in management, it can be a warning you haven't made the cut. Should you return from vacation and find your desk perched in a space that would crowd out a broom, take it as a "Scarlet Sign." Get out your résumé and pick up the phone.

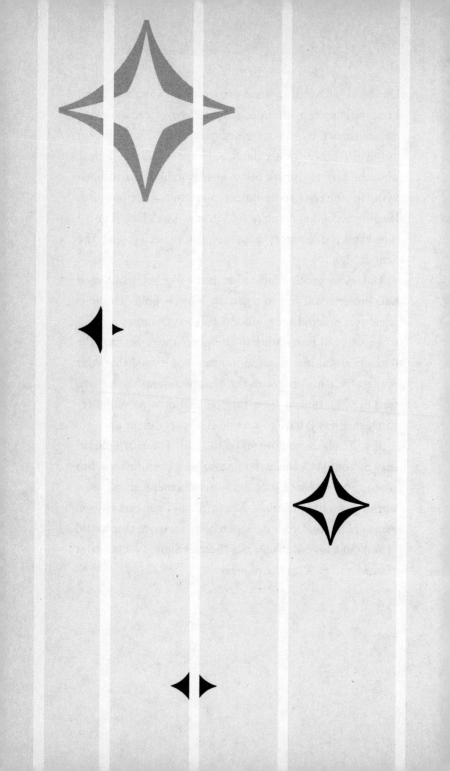

MARTYRS ARE REVERED
(BUT RARELY REWARDED)

It was hard not to dismiss Peggy as a drudge. With a doc-
torate in English literature, she was overqualified for the
job she took proofreading press releases and catalogues for
a Washington, D.C., museum. She thought that the job was
a starter position and that her diligence would soon be rewarded.

Peggy didn't see herself as others saw her—an unimag-
inative woman wearing ancient, pleated plaid skirts and
tailored white blouses, who was always bent over her desk,
pencil in hand, making little scratch marks on paper.
When others in the office asked her to join them in the
cafeteria for lunch, Peggy would shake her head, pointing
to the waiting manuscripts. Then she would open the bottom drawer of her desk, take out a brown paper bag, and,
reaching inside, extract the inevitable tuna-fish sandwich.
Peggy's manner tagged her as someone you could always
count on and, though no one ever actually said it, someone
you could take advantage of. But while her co-workers dis-

missed her as a woman who was dedicating her life to cleaning up others' grammatical mistakes, Peggy was living in a fantasy. She was not just making scratch marks on paper, she was conceiving and arranging exhibits of her own. Someday soon, instead of correcting catalogues, she would be writing them.

This dream drove Peggy to arrive at work an hour early each morning. By the time her boss turned up at nine, her desk held a neat pile of corrected proofs. As is the way in most offices, the more Peggy got done, the more she was given to do. Peggy acknowledges that she might have gone on like that for years, uncomplaining, convinced that people's admiration for her hard work would eventually lift her to another level.

Then, one day, she had an early-morning dentist appointment. By the time she arrived at the museum, her mouth still numb from novocaine, it was nine o'clock, and Peggy found herself riding up in the elevator with her boss. His "Good morning" was chilly, but Peggy wasn't prepared for the call she received from his secretary saying the boss wanted to see her, or for the reprimand she received for coming in "late."

"It was my own fault," Peggy admitted to Alexandra when they met at an opening at the museum and Peggy told Alexandra the source of her own Magic Words. "No one asked me to work all those hours. I should have used that time to advance myself in other ways—thinking up new ideas. It took me almost a year to wipe out the image I'd created of the automaton. But I did, and eventually I was offered a better job. A friend who'd listened to my woes did a little two-sided drawing for me. On one side there's a woman standing up against a wall, her arms crossed over her breasts while a lion approaches. It says 'Martyrs Are Revered.' On the flip side it says, 'But Rarely Rewarded,' and there's the lion, trotting off with the woman in his mouth. Believe me, those are Magic Words."

THE TRUMPET IS
A DANGEROUS INSTRUMENT

When we were little, we wanted instant praise for the things we accomplished, whether it was tying a shoelace or getting a gold star on a school paper. To make sure we got it, we issued the proud proclamation: "Look what I did."

As we got older, we learned not to demand praise. We were told that it was called bragging, and that braggarts weren't liked. The polite thing was to wait quietly and hope others noticed that we'd just won a Nobel Prize.

We learned to live in the middle zone—between the one where people fade into the wallpaper and the one where people brazenly flash their accomplishments with the insistence of a neon sign. Martyrdom is not good management, but neither is blowing your own horn. Alexandra and Howard learned long ago that "The Trumpet Is a Dangerous Instrument."

One time a friend invited Alexandra down to a weekend her ad agency had scheduled at a South Carolina fishing lodge. Among the other guests was one of the agency's sales executives. At breakfast, lunch, and dinner, the man talked of his skill at fly-fishing. He was, he said over and over, an incredible fisherman. By the time the party broke up, he had made a name for himself that spread far beyond his division—the name was "braggart," though a few suggested that an equally suitable moniker would be "bore."

The fly fisherman falls into Category One of the horn blowers we've encountered. He's obvious. He brags about himself.

There is also a Category Two in the brass section of the band: people who brag about someone else. A woman Alexandra once worked with was the mother of the Most Wonderful Child in the World, a juvenile paragon who, should the discussion stray to mountain climbing, was reported to be thinking of scaling Mount Everest. If the conversation moved on to cooking, the Most Wonderful Child in the World was preparing sauces far tastier than anything Emeril had devised. Category Two also contains the underling who gains stature by working for the Most Talented Man (or Woman) in the World. What these two braggarts have in common is that they're trumpeting the virtues of someone they're closely connected to. For them, bragging is a way of claiming gilt by association.

So how do you stop yourself from playing in the band? First pay attention to the way you behave. Are you like Annie Oakley in the musical *Annie Get Your Gun,* always insisting, "Anything You Can Do, I Can Do Better"? Do you listen to others' achievements impatiently, waiting for a break in the conversation so you can recount your own?

These are the actions of someone more interested in taking credit than in giving it. When talk of others' successes makes you want to brag about your own, remember that self-promotion in your job should lie in the middle zone. "The Trumpet Is a Dangerous Instrument"—and careers progress faster when the sound is turned down to pianissimo.

Unless you're Miles Davis, and he didn't need to brag.

YOUR SHIP CAN'T COME IN
IF IT HASN'T SET SAIL

Alexandra has a friend who's always thinking about what to do when he wins the lottery. Several years after she had first begun hearing of these fabulous plans, Alexandra discovered by chance that the future millionaire had never actually bought a lottery ticket. "It's too much trouble," the friend explained. "You have to wait for them to have the drawing to find out if you won."

When it comes to lottery tickets, the friend was probably right. He had the pleasure of fantasizing, and only a little less chance of winning than those who actually bought a ticket. But in most of life's endeavors, "Your Ship Can't Come In If It Hasn't Set Sail."

Eric is a prime example of a man standing on the dock watching an empty horizon. His dream is to move out of middle management, where he is currently stalled, and into the upper echelons of his company. Eric seems to feel that this event will happen by magic.

Last year, his company selected half a dozen people to

take a weeklong course at a prestigious business school. Eric's boss approached him to see if he'd be interested. Absolutely, said Eric, but not *that* week. That's when he'd planned to take several days off to go ice fishing up north. Needless to say, this year no one approached Eric about taking the course that might boost him into a more responsible job.

Lily is also stuck on the dock. When she inherited money from her grandmother, she decided to start her own business. So far, she has done intensive studies on the risks and rewards of opening a restaurant, a bookstore, a specialty-food store, a gallery selling crafts, and a frame shop. There are risks to everything, a friend has pointed out, and though it's sensible to evaluate a business before setting out, Lily's fear is likely to keep her ship on its mooring.

In the great days of the sailing ships, people knew that a voyage might bring a fortune or the ship might founder. A sound ship, a competent crew, and knowledge of the seas could reduce the risk, but the only way to ensure that a ship never sank was to keep it in dry dock. For those who took the risks, there were huge rewards; many New England families still rest on fortunes earned in the era when the ships came in. Taking a chance is part of life. Whether it is extending yourself at the job in hopes of improving your position, or taking a risk on a relationship that may not work out, these Magic Words will give you the courage to start your voyage.

YOU MEAN
IT'S NOT FUN ANYMORE?

Carrie was telling Alexandra about a man she worked for not long after she left college, a man who used humor to make the most tedious chore fly by. A year after she began working for him, he received a major promotion, which took him into the upper echelons of his company. Not long after he'd departed for a larger office on a higher floor, Carrie began to find it hard to get up in the morning. Now that she had become a manager herself, work, which was once a pleasure, had become a chore. Several weeks later, her former boss called and invited her to lunch. He was curious about how things were going in his old department.

Carrie said she almost wailed when she told him, "It's not so much fun anymore!" Then, fearing that she'd sounded childish and whiny, she quickly added, "That was a stupid thing to say. I mean, it *is* work. I know it's not supposed to be fun."

She was surprised by his reply—and his concern. "Of

course it's supposed to be fun. If you don't enjoy your work, you're not going to do it well."

Carrie told Alexandra that she'd never forgotten the man or that conversation. She began to think about how much of our lives we all spend at our work. Should she—or anyone else, for that matter—settle for forty hours a week on a job that wasn't enjoyable?

She told Alexandra that was the period in her life when she came up with her Magic Words—"You Mean It's Not Fun Anymore?"—and a strategy for change.

First, said Carrie, she adopted the philosophy passed on to generations of youngsters by Mrs. Piggle-Wiggle, the imaginative heroine of a series of children's books. When Mrs. Piggle Wiggle was faced with tedious household chores, she pretended to be a princess enslaved by a witch. Carrie said that everyone knows the witch always loses in the end, and that often it only takes a little make-believe to get through the difficult tasks that come with even the best of jobs.

When making a game of the tedious times didn't turn work into fun, Carrie said, she moved to part two of her strategy: she sought out the source of her unhappiness. Sometimes the problem was the work itself. Not all professions are for life. After many years of pursuing one line of work, people may burn out and need to move on to another. But when Carrie thought about what was making the days dreary, she realized it wasn't what she was doing but whom she was doing it for—executives who encouraged cutthroat competition and failed to praise employees for work well done. There's no point in changing jobs until you figure out whether it's the work you hate, or the people you do it for.

Carrie has many employees working under her these days, and she says she tries to make work fun. "Good humor, fairness, appreciating what people do on the job—all of that helps to make a job enjoyable. That and a spirit of play. I don't mean turning an office into a kindergarten, but understanding that we often get a lot more done when we're having a good time."

GRADUATE WITH HONORS

Anyone who's been stuck in a terrible job dreams of the day he or she can leave. Imagining the farewell speech—which will naturally peg the boss with such descriptive phrases as "baboon-faced" and "beer-bellied"—has gotten many a miserable serf through a really bad day.

Fortunately, getting a new job makes most people so happy that they forget all about their thirst for revenge. And that's as well, since careers can be affected by the way you leave a job as well as by the way you do one.

Take Peter. He was the manager of an inn in western Connecticut, and one day he simply disappeared. That was bad enough, but Peter had kept a record of reservations and employee hours on his personal computer. That, too, was gone. For several weeks, people who arrived at the inn learned their reservations had been lost; the inn did its best to accommodate everyone. Meanwhile, the owner prayed that the help was honest and that no one had taken advantage of the missing time sheets to claim extra hours.

He is still nursing his own dream of revenge. One day he hopes he'll receive a letter asking to recommend Peter for another job. Unless he learns before then that Peter was unconscious in a hospital bed when he failed to appear, he greatly looks forward to composing his reply.

Contrast that with Andrew, who was fired when his company had a bad year and cut back its staff. The manner of his firing was neither pleasant nor personal. His name was one of fifty on a list sent through the office. It arrived before the e-mail telling him that he would receive a month's pay in lieu of notice. Andrew was upset, but he was smart enough to write an upbeat letter to the head of his division, saying how much he had enjoyed working for the company. A year later, Andrew got a call asking if he'd come back. Still friendly, Andrew said that he had another job and that he was content where he was, but he thanked the man for calling. Andrew says that when his career frustrates and angers him he takes his anger to the squash court. In the office, he smiles.

Think of the office the way you would a social situation. Everyone has sat through dinners where the food was inedible and the talk tedious. You may have wondered if the evening would ever end, but on leaving, you didn't tell your hostess you'd had a terrible time and wished her the worst. That's partly because we've been raised to be polite, and partly because no one wants to earn a reputation as a difficult guest. Think how much more devastating it would be if the professional world you work in marked you off as a difficult person to work with.

When you say "so long," add "it's been good to know you." "Graduating with Honors" means treating the people you leave behind with courtesy and kindness. It's good manners, and it's good business. You never know when you'll need someone's help.

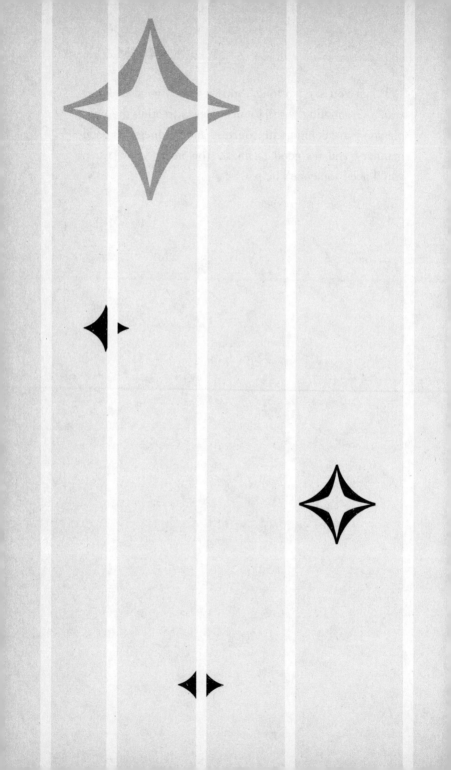

"Toys for boys," Alexandra muttered, as the sleek Porsche slid through the yellow light and made its way down Madison Avenue. Louise, with whom she had been lunching, laughed harder than the comment called for.

"Why so funny?" Alexandra asked.

"Because you've just described Jeff," said Louise, "or, rather, the old Jeff, before I finally figured out a way to stop him from acquiring every toy and gadget in the universe. Sports cars were bad enough—did we really need two? And the boat. And the tractor. Not a little lawn tractor, but a full-sized John Deere. I finally asked Jeff's mother whether his first words were 'Vrooom! Vrooom!' Apparently he was an acquisition freak from birth. But the worst part was that his lust for new toys had begun to hurt his company. Anytime he'd go to a trade show, he'd write an order for some piece of equipment that the company really didn't need. If one of the trade journals had an article on a new way to package products, he'd call and make an appointment with the salesman. And, of course, he'd sign a contract to install the new system.

"Profits were being plowed back into unnecessary equipment," continued Louise, who knew as much about the company as Jeff, since it had come to them through her father. "My dad was very conservative about adding new things. He grew up in New Hampshire, and when we were little he used to admonish us, 'Use it up, wear it out, make it do, or do without.' Actually, he went too far, and many of the changes Jeff made when we inherited the company were absolutely necessary to keep us competitive. I guess the two of them were at opposite extremes: Jeff is too ac-quisitive, and my father was too thrifty. I thought it was time that we moved toward the middle—not getting things just because they were new, but not ignoring advances that would help the company.

"I was trying to think of a way to get this across to Jeff when I remembered something else about my father. He was death on catalogues. They went into the wastebasket before any of us had a chance to see them. He'd say, 'What the eyes don't see, the heart don't yearn for.' And I thought if there was some way to keep Jeff from seeing all these shiny toys he wouldn't buy them.

"So I sat Jeff down and made a suggestion. For one year, as a trial, he'd agree not to go to trade shows, and someone would screen the trade journals, clipping articles of inter-est to the company and passing them along to him. No ads. Someone else would be given the job of evaluating any new equipment that came on the market and reporting to the board. I told Jeff that if he agreed we'd reward him with an end-of-the-year toy of choice. I figured that if we could keep him from spending too much on unnecessary equipment we could even afford a Porsche.

"Jeff agreed. He's not stupid, and he knew he was an easy mark. He just didn't know how to stop.

"Now, here's the interesting part. For an entire year, instead of buying something he'd just seen, Jeff shopped for ideas. He wanted to get the very best toy as his reward. For the first time in his life, he actually did some research on things. Once he knew he'd get one really big plaything—but only one—he became a critical shopper. One week it would be a sports car. The next he'd be convinced the toy should be a new boat.

"Here's the kicker. The company had a great year. Sure, we bought some new equipment, but things we needed. Not just stuff because it was new. And I made a big deal out of how well he'd done. We went out to dinner, and I handed him a wrapped package. He opened it, and inside there was a slip of paper. 'Toys "R" You.' I told him it was good for whatever he really wanted. You'll never believe what he chose. A fishing camp! My husband the consumer. He said that after an entire year of contemplating every toy he might have had, he'd begun to realize that he hadn't been spending money on things he really wanted, but on things the advertisers had convinced him he wanted. Of course," Louise added with a twinkle in her eye, "he also wanted really good tackle."

Louise says that since the year when her husband

learned that postponing what you get can teach you what you want, he's been back at the trade shows, and so far he hasn't bought a single thing. Meanwhile, he's learned that toys are for "boys," and essentials are what make corporations make money.

Alexandra learned these Magic Words years ago, when an editor assigned her to interview a writer who was notoriously spare with the spoken word. "I'm dying to meet him," she confessed, "but how am I going to get him to say anything?"

"You mean you've never practiced 'The Sphinx Effect'?" the editor asked.

Alexandra admitted that not only had she never practiced it, she didn't know what it was.

"Instead of trying to keep the conversation going, just ask your question, and if he answers it with a single 'yes,' don't jump in and ask another. Sit there quietly waiting, as mysterious and inscrutable as the sphinx. People grow uncomfortable when a conversation stops. They jump in to keep it going. If you stay silent and wait for a longer, fuller answer, you'll usually get it. Your silence compels the other person to speak."

Alexandra used "The Sphinx Effect" in many an awkward interview, and she found that the editor was right:

silence drew out the other person in ways that repeated questioning would not.

When she mentioned the technique to her friend Edward, she learned that he, too, practiced it, but quite differently from her. Edward is in the U.S. diplomatic service, and he said that one of the first things he learned was when to be silent. "I was in our embassy in a small Third World country that shall be nameless and had been asked to set up a meeting between a large U.S. manufacturer and the country's president and his trade advisers. The manufacturer, which wanted to open a plant in the region, had obviously made a poor choice in their negotiator—they sent a vice-president who was only a step away from thinking he'd get the rights for a handful of beads. Our ambassador was concerned the man would offend the country's president; he asked me to meet with the negotiator first, to try to explain the situation.

"The man arrived at my office and immediately began to lecture me on the way to do business in 'these places.' He ranted on for upwards of half an hour before he noticed that I hadn't said anything. 'You agree, of course?' he asked. I still didn't say anything. I just looked at him, and then I pulled a pad of paper over and made a few notes. He tried to see what I'd written, but the angle was wrong. 'Well, *don't* you agree?' He was sounding a little less sure.

" 'You've spent time in this country, of course,' I said, making it a statement, as though I couldn't imagine he'd be going on like this if he hadn't.

"He blustered, 'You don't have to spend time here to know what these people want.'

"Again, I didn't say anything. I just made another note on my pad.

" 'Don't you think it will work?'

"I shrugged.

"At this point he was getting frantic. The president and his advisers were due to arrive in fifteen minutes. He finally asked, 'Well, what do *you* think we should offer?'

"Finally I began to talk. I told him a bit about the president's background. That he'd gone to Oxford. That he really did care about improving the economic situation in his country. That he had a reputation for honesty and was proud, not a man likely to respond well to the offer of a bribe. I suggested that instead of offering the deal he'd come with, he consider this a preliminary meeting, one where he simply listened to what the president had to say. And that's the meeting we had. The negotiator returned a month later with a realistic offer, and the company got its plant.

"If I had tried to tell him he was going at it the wrong way, he wouldn't have listened. The sphinx approach made him uncomfortable. My silence got across the idea that something was wrong, but he didn't know what. I made him doubt himself, and that made him ready to listen to what I had to say."

Alexandra has since learned that there are other reasons to be silent: to learn what everyone else has to say before you add your own ideas, to be able to point out the flaw in someone's earlier argument, to develop a reputation as a person who only speaks when there is something important to say, and, of course, to be generous enough to let other people have the floor.

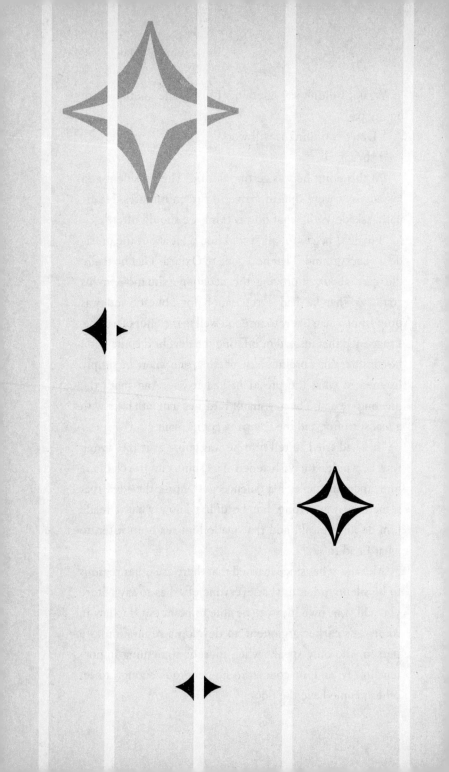

GO ON THE
SILVER STANDARD

Go for the gold? In our day-to-day lives full of divergent demands, we may be wiser to settle for silver.

Howard's friend Frank put himself on the gold standard and it almost cost him his company and career. Frank always aimed for the top, giving any project his total concentration. But while Frank had his focus fixed on the peak, problems would grow in the valleys below. It was as if Frank had never heard of the term "multitasking" and seemed unable to understand that it's something managers must know how to do.

Frank had quit his job with a publishing firm to set up an imprint of his own—a house that would bring back into print books whose copyrights had expired. Frank's obvious first task was to develop the list of books he would offer for sale, but, wrapped up in his desire to find the very best, he made that his only task. Frank had a fantasy that he would find brilliant books that had been ignored the first time around. Instead of making obvious choices, he shut himself up with ancient book reviews, looking for out-of-print books that could become instant classics.

Which was all very well, but while Frank looked for stars shining out from the past, he neglected the other parts of his business. He postponed making the necessary arrangements with a printer and distributor. He failed to make the phone calls and lunch dates that would keep his backers happy. The company Frank had started so hopefully would probably have died without publishing a single book if Howard hadn't taken him out to lunch.

As they ate at a new gourmet hot spot, Frank enthused about an obscure cookbook by a famous author that he'd recently discovered. When Howard asked him about other aspects of the business, Frank admitted to having fallen behind. "But I'm going to have the best list any reprint house ever had," he boasted.

"You're going to have nothing," Howard rejoined. "Let me tell you something about going for the gold. It's mostly athletes who do it, and you know why they can? Because someone else runs their lives and leaves them free to concentrate on only one thing. I have a friend whose daughter is an athlete. Do you know that her manager not only buys her clothes, he sends someone in to cut her hair? She has only one thing to do—to train constantly, so that she'll excel. Frank, you're not an athlete. You're a businessman, and that means doing the best you can at a variety of things. If you give a hundred percent to only one thing, you've got zilch for the others. It's business triage, Frank. Each day, you have to decide what's the most important thing to do, and do it. Sometimes you'll manage to make it gold, but most days, to do it all, you're going to have to 'Go on the Silver Standard.' "

Frank listened to Howard and—reluctantly, it has to be said—began to wean himself away from a list stuffed with out-of-print blockbusters. Frank's book list, when it appeared, was a good one. Most of the books will have a steady sale, and there are one or two that Howard thinks may well become gold-standard classics. Like the rest of us, Frank had to learn to organize his priorities. On some items you can go for the gold, but to get everything done, wise people settle for silver.

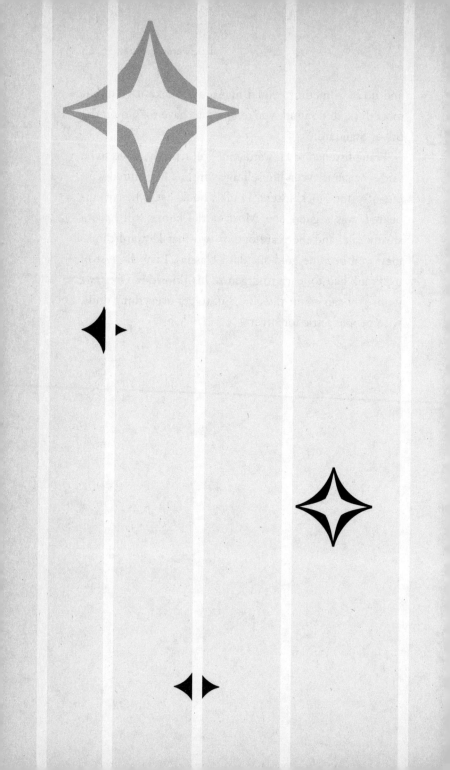

THE TWO-STONE SOLUTION

You are as unlikely to kill a bird with a single stone as you are to solve a problem with a single solution. Not that we recommend pelting birds, but you get the idea. The wise hunter, whether faced with prey or with problems, goes forth well armed.

Both of us use "The Two-Stone Solution" whenever we're faced with a dilemma. And we never go into a meeting with a single solution to the problem at hand. We know how easy it is for someone else to see the flaw we failed to notice. So we pack up our two stones and remember Bert, the man who gave us these Magic Words and the story that went with them.

Bert runs a major pest-control business, and though he franchises the service and is not likely to be seen tiptoeing through a back garden carrying a Havaheart trap, he has an endless stream of stories from the field.

Our favorite involved an oven and a squirrel.

"A young fellow named Curtis, who had just bought one

of our Connecticut franchises, called me with a problem. It seems some woman had asked him to come out because she was sure there were animals living in her attic, or scurrying up and down behind the walls, leaving, shall we say, 'droppings' in their wake. Curtis checked out the attic, and even though he didn't see any of the usual signs, he set a trap. A few days later, he went back. The trap was empty, but the woman was insistent that there was an animal problem. There was a smell, she said, and it was getting worse. I should tell you that, each time Curtis arrived, the woman met him at the front door and took him right up to the attic. So Curtis set another trap, baiting it with peanut butter and raisins. Best bait there is, by the way. Again, no luck. The woman was getting angry, and Curtis called me.

"He said he was getting so frustrated that now when he went to check the trap he put his slingshot in his pocket. 'I know we're supposed to catch and release, but if I ever see this squirrel I'm going to have my slingshot ready.'

" 'So, Curtis, you've got a stone in your pocket?'

" 'Yep.'

" 'Well, I think you'd better get yourself a different stone, 'cause that one isn't going to solve your problem.'

"Curtis asked what I meant, and I told him that he'd let that lady define the problem for him, and that meant she'd also dictated his solution: Trap the squirrel. Stone it. So I asked Curtis if he had any appointments that afternoon. He didn't. I told him to drive out to the lady's house, skip the attic, and go into the kitchen. 'Look in the oven,' I said, 'and then call me back.'

"Well, he was mighty embarrassed when he called. When he'd opened the oven door he'd almost passed out. There was the stinking remnant of a two-week-old roast chicken. I said, 'Curtis, always carry two stones. One for the problem people think they have, the other for the problem you take the trouble to find.' Curtis thinks I'm a genius. I didn't tell him that, in all the years I've been in the pest-control business, the biggest cause of animal odors has been meat that got left in the oven."

MANAGING SHOULDER
TO SHOULDER

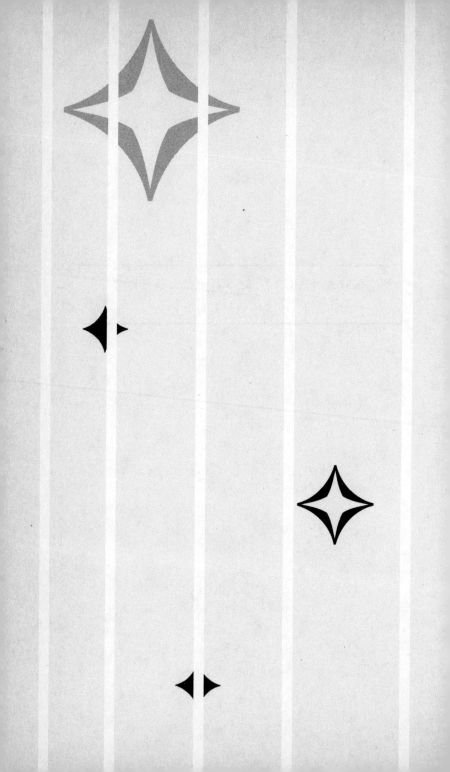

DON'T WEIGH THE FACTS
WITH YOUR THUMB ON THE SCALE

Alexandra found herself sitting next to Gus at dinner not long after the stock market had gone into free fall. The other guests were singing a single chorus—a dirge of stocks gone south and money vanished. Except Gus, who sat there smiling and looking smug. "What have you got to look so happy about?" Alexandra asked. Gus looked thoughtful for a minute and then said, "I guess I'm happy because my grandfather was a butcher."

Needless to say, that was an intriguing response, and Alexandra pursued it. "A few years ago," said Gus, "a friend called and turned me on to a new company. He was raising capital for a group that, he insisted, had found a way to make a fortune on the Internet. I won't bore you with the details—they're all too familiar right now. I had decided to buy in. Half the people I knew seemed to be minting money, buying stocks that would double in a couple of months. I guess we all believed that this was our genera-tion's big chance, sort of like buying into the early movie industry, or radio or TV back in the days when they were just starting up. Did I sincerely want to be rich? I did. But before I committed myself to how much I was willing to invest, I went out to my parents' house for the weekend. Sitting around on Saturday, I told my father about the new company; I thought he might want to come in on it with me. Before I went back to the city on Sunday, I gave him the prospectus and a lot of other financial information I'd gathered. On Tuesday I was walking up Madison Avenue, on my way to meet someone for lunch, when my cell phone rang. I answered, and I heard my father's gravelly voice saying, 'The grandson of a butcher should know better than to weigh things with his thumb on the scale.'

"My grandfather started out as a butcher," Gus explained. "Though he eventually built up a wholesale-meat company, he always made sure we remembered where the money had come from. So I guess I really knew what my father was saying, but I went ahead and asked, 'What do you mean?'

" 'You wanted this company to be good,' he said. 'You couldn't wait to get in on the Internet bonanza, and so you're seeing things that just aren't there. This company is going to be a dud. Put your money in bonds.' I took my father's advice," said Gus. "That's why I'm smiling."

And that's why we are passing along Gus's Magic Words. Whenever you, or one of your colleagues, wants a business deal so badly that you let your greed skew your judgment, it's time to remember the butcher's advice: "Don't Weigh the Facts with Your Thumb on the Scale."

It's not surprising that Joan's Magic Words involve food. Joan is a successful caterer working in a medium-sized Midwestern city who adopted them the year she almost lost her business.

Although she is an excellent cook, Joan had no specialized culinary training. She learned the business from the bottom up from a local caterer, a woman named Vivian who specialized in the kinds of food that had been popular in the late 1960s and early '70s—melted Brie sprinkled with almonds and served with French bread, beef Wellington for that very special occasion. Vivian's menu may have been caught in a time warp, but her clients were drawn from her own generation, and she always turned a profit. In between teaching Joan how to encase beef in pâté and brioche, Vivian taught her how to run a business.

When Vivian died, she left Joan the company, and Joan, thrilled with the windfall, decided to aim for a larger audience. A friend introduced her to Nina, who had trained as a chef in France, and who had the money to pay for a partnership. Two months into the new arrangement, Joan's windfall was becoming a pratfall. As creative as Nina was with cooking, she couldn't meet the deadlines that come with catering.

"I didn't know what to do," says Joan, remembering the tension of that time. "We'd used Nina's money to expand, and I couldn't afford to buy her out. I was working harder than ever to make up for Nina's slowness. A man I'd been dating stopped by one night to complain that he never saw me anymore—I was always in the kitchen. I explained the predicament and said I was in a pickle. When I said that, it reminded me that Nina wanted me to try a new pâté she'd made. It was on a plate in the refrigerator, surrounded by slices of sweet gherkin. My friend readily accepted the pâté but shook his head when I topped it with a sliced gherkin. He said he didn't like foods that were sour. 'Not all pickles are sour,' I said, offering it again. And then I heard what I'd said.

"Maybe I had been too ready to accept that the situation with Nina was sour. Maybe I needed to think how to make it sweet."

Joan did work it out. She realized that she had been looking at the downside of Nina's talent, the time it took for her to prepare new and unusual dishes. Now the day-to-day cooking is done by Joan and an employee she calls "the other workhorse." Nina runs the creative end, consulting with clients and keeping the menu fresh and imaginative.

"Learning to see things differently turned my life around," says Joan. "I learned that if you want a happy life it pays to look at things from several angles. It's not just at work that a negative may turn out to be a positive. Several years ago, when I bought my first house, I couldn't afford what I really wanted. I settled for a place that had a lot of flaws—it was definitely a sour pickle. But those very flaws led to creative solutions. Today you couldn't pry me out of my sour-pickle house. It's home sweet home."

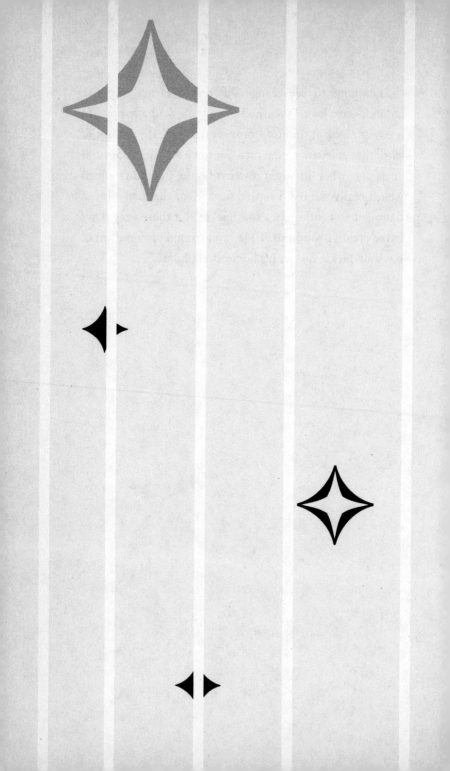

"She was late for her own wedding!" Stanley said to Alexandra, his voice rising to a near shout as he tried to explain the difficulty he'd had with a woman he concedes helped make his public-relations business the success it is. Alexandra remembered how excited Stanley had been when Leah had first joined the company some ten years before, how he'd considered her a major boon to his fledgling firm. Leah was off-the-wall creative, a woman who'd once managed to get a mass-media magazine to run a story on Stanley's dullest client by having the client stroll around the Lower East Side of New York handing out coins to teenagers. Leah had instructed the client to begin with dimes, and then raise the ante until the teens expressed gratitude instead of derision. It was, she had convinced the magazine, which had a photographer following along, a way to measure how our currency had become inflated since the days of John D. Rockefeller.

Stanley loved the woman he called "the dime dame,"

THE GRACE SPACE ✦ 78

but her inability to meet a deadline drove him crazy. "Do you know why it's called a deadline?" Stanley asked Alexandra.

"Because if you don't get the piece in on time the editor will shoot you," Alexandra volunteered.

"Exactly," said Stanley. "But not an editor. It's from the Civil War, from Andersonville Prison, the horrible camp for captured Confederate soldiers. There was a stockade fence around the camp, and seventeen feet farther out they had marked out another line. Any prisoner who crossed that final line was shot on sight. It was, naturally, called the deadline."

"So—are you going to shoot Leah?"

"Maybe," said Stanley, and changed the subject.

The next time Alexandra saw Stanley, she brought up the subject of Leah.

"Did you ever get things worked out?" she asked.

"I did," said Stanley. "I got to thinking about that original deadline and how it had real meaning for those prisoners. But I also thought about that extra seventeen feet, a sort of grace space. It wasn't until they crossed the final line that the prisoners were shot. Since Leah's always been good at coming up with creative solutions to problems, I called her into my office. I thought I'd get her to come up with a solution to her own missed deadlines.

"I asked her why it was so hard for her to get things in on time. She thought a long while, and finally she said, 'I'm never satisfied with what I've done. I want to give you the best, and I hold on as long as I can, thinking that maybe I'll come up with a better idea.'

"So I told her about the origin of the term 'deadline,' and I mentioned that I couldn't get the idea of that grace space out of my head. Seventeen feet that could keep you from dying. Leah got as fascinated as I was, and it led her to come up with a solution that worked so well for her that now we make it standard office practice.

"We have two time frames: the fence and the deadline. Say you're working on a proposal for promoting a cruise line. We'll assign you a fence. That means your rough ideas are due on February 1. Then you get a deadline, which is seventeen days past that. The grace space between the fence and the deadline is the time when I get a chance to look at what you've done and make suggestions. It works because no one on the staff feels pressured to produce a finished product. They've got extra time to make improvements."

"So," Alexandra asked, "what do you do when someone misses the deadline?"

"No one has yet," said Stanley, "but if they do they all know I'll shoot them."

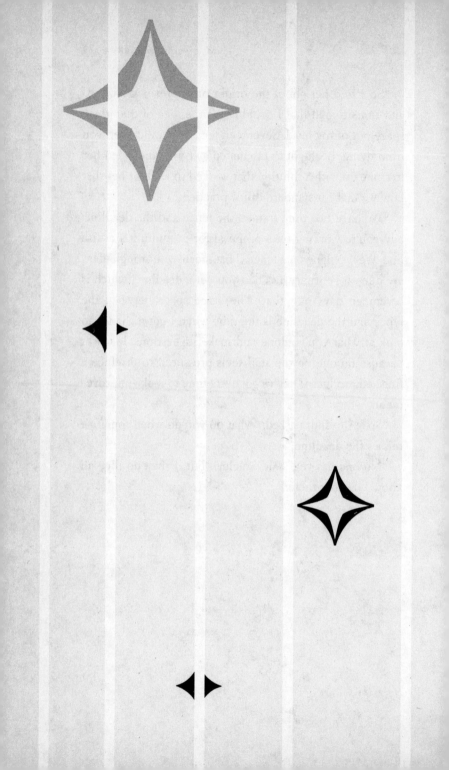

YOU CAN'T FOCUS
FROM TOO FAR AWAY

The idea was simple. While other boys had been working on cars, both Bob and Greg had spent their teen years in basement workshops, learning the art of woodworking. Both now lived in small city apartments where they had no space to pursue their hobby.

"What if we jointly rent a room somewhere?" Bob suggested, and Greg took the idea a step further. "What if we rent a whole shop? There must be a lot of guys like us who have no space to work. We could provide the place and the tools, charge by the hour, or maybe have people sign up for membership."

The idea grew. They'd start with two shops. Bob would manage one, Greg the other, and then they'd expand into other neighborhoods throughout the city. They named their new company Work Away, and Bob hired a lawyer to handle the legal problems. The two men scouted sites, checked out fire regulations, looked into what insurance they'd need to carry, what it would cost to advertise, and whether it made more sense to charge by the hour or to sell memberships.

And then, folders brimming with information, friends lined up to help with additional financing and the choice of four possible sites, they decided they needed a break to clear their heads before they plunged in deeper. Bob headed out to Sun Valley for two weeks of skiing. Greg went to Buenos Aires.

Away from each other, isolated from the mutual enthusiasm that had made anything possible, they both began to have doubts. On his return, Greg wondered aloud if they'd taken on too much. What if the idea failed? Greg's concerns added to the fears Bob had begun to feel. A partnership works both ways. Sometimes one shores up the other, but when both partners weaken at the same time, the structure crumbles.

And so Bob and Greg gave up.

Any new business venture is a risk. So are old business ventures, and even the safest job is never entirely secure. Companies fail, demand for a product changes, poor business practices take down even a giant like the accounting firm of Arthur Andersen. But those risks are minimized by a very clear focus on the business at hand. Football teams can surge into the lead with a brilliant kickoff return, and then, after the half, slack off and lose the game. A passion for any venture has to start with the kickoff, and it has to continue until the final down.

"We put in over six months' work on our plans," Bob says today. "Up to that point, we'd done everything right.

Taking a break was a bad idea; we lost our momentum. We told ourselves that we were just getting some perspective, but we really lost our focus. Not long after we'd put things on hold, Greg's firm transferred him to the West Coast. That was the end of Work Away."

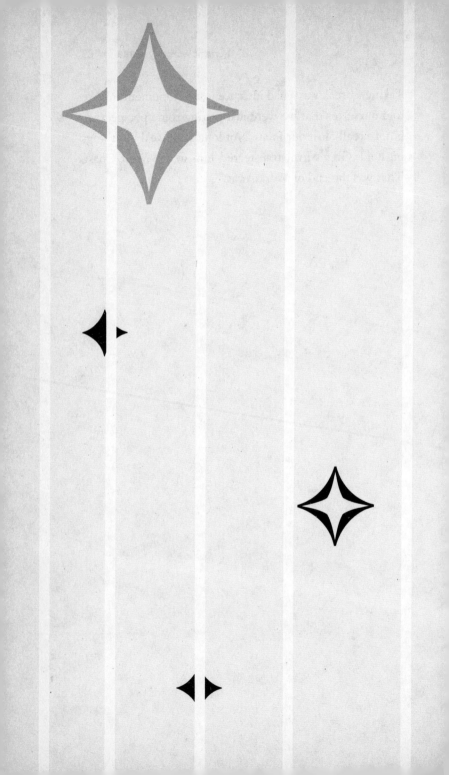

Howard was twenty-seven when he was given his first managerial post. Granted, he had only two people under him (and one was his secretary), but he was (sound of drums here, please) a *manager*. Even though it wasn't like becoming the chairman of a Fortune 500 company, for Howard it was a big thing. Then, less than a month after he'd been raised to this exalted position, a scandal ripped through the office. It was the equivalent of 8.4 on the Richter scale: someone had discovered that the head of the publishing house had cooked the books to the tune of two million dollars.

Needless to say, the board of directors immediately fired the CEO and asked Brad, who had been chief operating officer, to take over his job temporarily. The betting in the company was that Brad's new position would become permanent, and that meant, said the office gossips, that someone in-house was probably going to be named COO. Everyone agreed that the logical candidate was

Howard's immediate boss, Glenn, who, in addition to Howard's micro-operation, managed three other departments in the publishing house.

The gossips weren't alone in thinking Glenn would get the job. So did Glenn, who put everything else aside and began a full-time lobbying campaign. There were talks over coffee, one-on-one lunches, drinks, and dinner parties centered around anyone in the company he thought might help him get the job. In those spare moments he had when he wasn't lobbying, Glenn drafted plans on how he'd restructure the company.

It wasn't long before word of Glenn's activities reached Brad, who casually dropped by his office for a chat.

"Glenn, how are things going?" he asked.

"You know. Busy, just the same old same old."

"That's not what I hear."

"What do you mean?"

"Seems like you've changed your job title."

"No, I haven't," said a confused Glenn.

"My understanding is you've become a full-time lobbyist. That's not what you were hired to do, Glenn."

Brad went on to tell Glenn that, with the company going through a rough time, it was important that everyone do his or her job well. "You're not thinking of the company, Glenn. You're thinking of your own gain. I don't think that's a good sign."

Brad said that there would be another meeting of the board of directors in two weeks, and that the board had assured him that he'd be named CEO. "My original plan was to ask them to name you to take over my old job. But your lack of concern for the company in these last two months has made me change my mind. I wanted you to hear it from me. I'm not recommending you."

A few weeks later, Glenn, who realized he'd ruined his chance of advancement with the company, left for another job.

When Howard had lunch with Brad several months later, Brad asked whether he ever heard from Glenn.

"I spoke to him last week," Howard said.

"I hope he's doing well. He's got a lot of ability. The only thing Glenn's got to learn is to do his exercises in the gym."

"What do you mean?"

"During the whole time the company was fighting off scandal, Glenn never did what he was paid to do. He came in every day and did push-ups, trying to push himself up into a better job. Instead of all for one and one for all, Glenn was all for himself. He thought he could take advantage of the company's bad luck to improve his position. I don't mean you shouldn't hope for a promotion. But the way to earn one is by doing what you're supposed to do and doing it well."

Since his first management job, Howard has worked in many places where problems in the company left positions to be filled. Someone else might have lobbied for promotion, but Howard always remembered what Brad had said. Work hard at the job you've got; "Push-Ups Belong in the Gym."

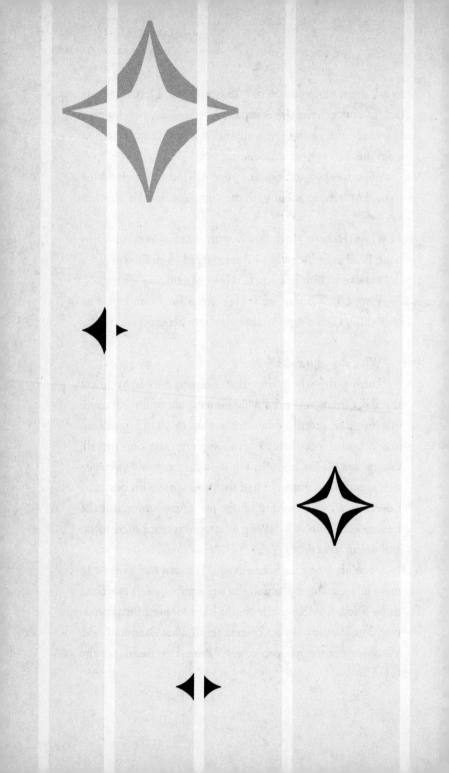

BURY THE HATCHET— IN THE COMPETITION

Question: why is having an ongoing dispute with a co-worker even worse than having one with your next-door neighbor? That's a no-brainer—you don't have to spend eight hours a day working alongside your neighbor!

Unfortunately, both of us have had protracted and messy arguments with officemates. A few times, they've stopped just short of pitched battles. They've been unpleasant and, worst of all, distracted us from what we were being paid to do. In most cases, we now reluctantly admit, we shared a fair amount of blame for the dispute. It took us a while to develop a way to handle these situations, but now when they arise we don't get even, we don't curse, we don't hide, we don't yell—we look for a place to bury the hatchet so that we won't use it on our co-worker.

"The first fight I had with Eddie was over something very small," Howard remembered, "like where we should have the office Christmas party. We were given the assignment by Bill, the man who ran the company, and it should have been easy, but it wasn't. Eddie wanted to hold it in a dance club in Chelsea, and I was all for a hot, new restaurant in the Village. Why the restaurant? Food, food, food. I love to eat, and I knew the food at the club was atrocious. I finally won out. But since people couldn't dance at the restaurant, the party was a very staid affair. I was the only one who really liked it. I gained three pounds gorging myself on bruschetta and tiramasù."

The Christmas contretemps was just the start of Howard's problems with Eddie. They were on the same level in the company, both running small divisions, which meant that they frequently had to work together. In addition, twice each day they attended the same meetings. For two people who didn't like each other, that was a lot of contact. Pretty soon they had another major disagreement, more serious than whether they should dance to celebrate Christmas or eat. This was about how to launch a new line of paperbacks. Before long they were engaging in shouting matches in front of their co-workers. At that point, Bill called Howard into his office.

"What gives with you and Eddie?"

"Nothing serious," Howard said. "We just don't always see eye to eye."

"Cut the bull, Howard. The two of you are worse than Tom Arnold and Roseanne Barr. This has to stop."

"Believe me, Bill, I'm working on it," Howard lied, knowing that the only thing he was working on was a fantasy that had Eddie giving notice and vanishing.

"Do."

That single syllable, and the curt way Bill said it, was a warning that he expected Howard to find some way to bury the hatchet—and fast. "Much as I longed to do it," Howard said, "I'd be in nothing but trouble if I followed my instincts and buried it in Eddie. For some reason, thinking about how I could make myself work with Eddie reminded me of a picnic when I was a kid. I was paired with a boy I hated in the three-legged race, and we had to find some way to run in sync or we'd come in last.

"In all our dealings, Eddie and I had been fighting each other for position inside the company. We'd never stood shoulder to shoulder fighting the competition. The place to bury the hatchet wasn't in each other but in the company that was beating us in sales."

Howard went back to Bill and suggested that Eddie and he do a joint report on what our competition was doing that we weren't. Suddenly, instead of looking for intraoffice enemies, they were looking outside the company. "It was still war, but now Eddie and I were on the same side," says Howard. "I'll never be close to Eddie. Someone said—though I hope it isn't true—that we're too much alike. But I learned that you can waste a lot of energy fighting a war inside the company. When you ask yourself, 'Where should I put this hatchet?' the intelligent answer is 'In the competition.' "

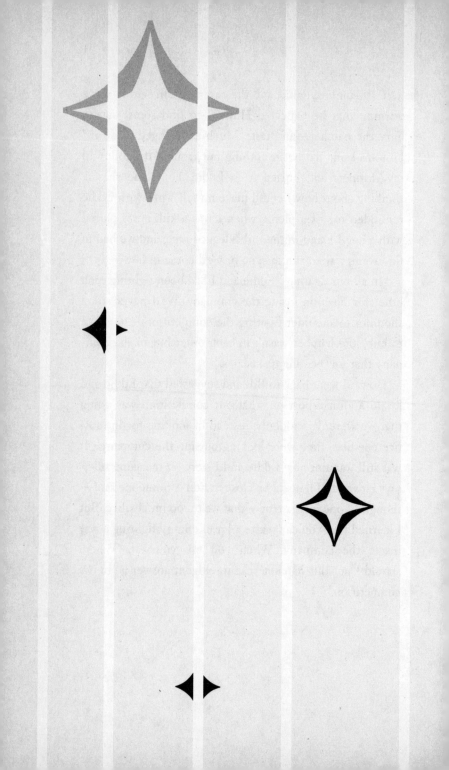

SNAP!
THEN THINK AGAIN

Alexandra had always thought of Laila as a softie, the kind of woman who feeds stray cats and tries to get you to believe that the reason your boyfriend forgot your birthday is that he's having trouble at his job.

So it didn't surprise her some years back when Laila told her that she had her own Magic Words. These, Laila said, were meant to keep her from making snap judgments about people who got under her skin. Laila, who works for an accounting firm, came up with them one day when a co-worker made fun of a suggestion she'd made at a meeting. "My first reaction was anger; then I thought again. Gordon—that's his name—is overweight, and my statement was about how overeating could affect people's health. I realized he'd taken it personally, thought I was getting at him. I'd been insensitive and he'd reacted. So I didn't snipe back. I went out of my way to be extra friendly, and what could have turned into an office feud faded away.

"Ever since then, whenever I start to get annoyed with

someone in the office, or feel that someone is stepping on my toes, I use my Magic Words: "Snap! Then Think Again." And I try to figure out if something is going on that's making the person behave this way. Sometimes it turns out to be something I've done. Sometimes I learn that the person is going through a hard time—a divorce, a parent diagnosed with cancer, a child who's gotten into drugs. These are all things that have happened to people in my division, and, believe me, when people are having personal problems they can be very, very touchy. When you think someone you work with is out to get you, it pays to think again. A little understanding can avoid a lot of unpleasantness."

After Laila had told her about "Think Again," Alexandra did just that. She had been offered an interesting job with an innovative company but was thinking of turning it down. Her reason was that she'd be working with a woman she'd once had an unpleasant argument with at a dinner party. When the woman's name had been mentioned, Alexandra's immediate thought had been, "Uh-oh, I don't like her." If that woman was there, did she want to be?

Now Alexandra followed Laila's suggestion. She thought again. As hard as she tried, she couldn't remember what the argument had been about. And hadn't she herself been rather touchy back then, trying to decide whether to end a difficult relationship?

Alexandra took the job, and on her first day in the new office she went up to the woman she had argued with so long ago, introduced herself, and said, "I hope you don't remember me, since the only time we met was at a dinner party where I involved you in a ridiculous argument. If you do remember me, I belatedly apologize. I know I'm going to like working with you, and I would hate it if you thought I was as stubborn as I was that night."

The woman, completely disarmed, offered to show Alexandra around. Because of the Magic Words, Alexandra didn't start her new job with an enemy, but with a friend—who also found it funny that they'd once argued so furiously and now neither could remember why.

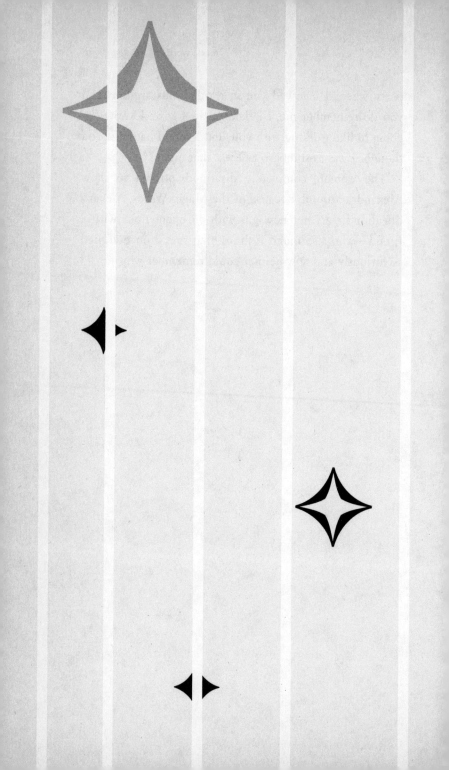

CIRCUIT BREAKERS

Our friend Marian has a collection of framed drawings in her library. Not Old Masters, these are humorous sketches of a character called Patchwork Pig, who cavorts his way through a series of adventures and always emerges triumphant.

When Alexandra asked Marian about the pig drawings, she said, "Patchwork was our office lifesaver." Marian, who headed the marketing department of an upscale textile company, explained that Patchwork had evolved among the staff as a way of letting off tension. "Whenever we were drowning, Patchwork Pig would come to the rescue. Someone would do a funny little drawing of Patchwork swimming out to a sinking ocean liner, or Patchwork untying a maiden wrapped in a roll of our fabric from a railway track. Whoever did the drawing would make Xerox copies of it and leave it on everyone's desks. Instead of getting into a complete panic about an approaching deadline or the cancellation of a major order, we'd let Patchwork come to the rescue. Patchwork put things in perspective, letting us laugh about the situation and move on to putting things right."

Marian's story illustrates one of Alexandra and Howard's favorite Magic Words, "Circuit Breakers," those devices used by office staff to keep from suffering overload.

The dot-com generation, with its flamboyantly casual management style, perfected the "circuit breaker" by making foosball tables part of the office equipment. The game, with little figures that send the balls flying back and forth, had been around for years under other names, but it took the techies to set it up next to the filing cabinets.

More conservative offices like to keep the "circuit breakers" out of sight, but an amazing number of businesses now offer gyms or exercise classes as a way of keeping employees from giving in to stress. When things get tense, think "Circuit Breaker," and if you haven't come up with your own, feel free to borrow these.

Howard once learned that members of his staff had set up an Office Olympics. When they needed to go to another floor, they called ahead, getting the person at the other end to start the stopwatch. Rules of the game banned running in the hallway or office—anywhere a top executive might be—but running on the stairs was okay. Everyone surmised that though you might encounter the CEO standing in a hall waiting for an elevator, you weren't likely to meet up in the stairwell. Howard never let on that he knew about it, but he thought Office Olympics a great way to work off tension. Not to mention that manuscripts and memos were delivered faster than the speed of light. And though he didn't officially know, once a month Howard had his secretary fill him in on the current scores.

Alexandra thinks she knows the ultimate "circuit breaker," provided by a member of her editorial department when she was editor of *Self* magazine. It was a sweet golden retriever who accompanied her owner to work. Members of the staff found reasons to drop by and stroke the dog's silky coat, and Alexandra, who knows because she did it herself, says it was a tension tamer better than a quick back rub or camomile tea.

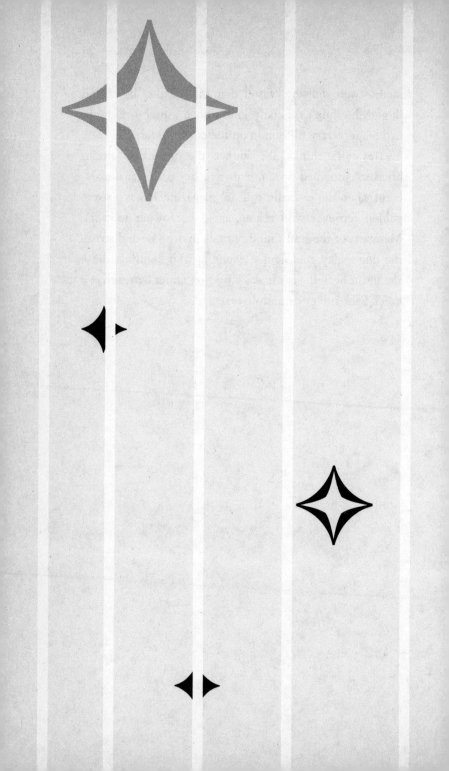

THUMBS CAN BE
PRETTY GOOD RULERS

Some years back, when Howard was the president of a publishing company, he got involved in a big auction for a first novel. Everybody in the house loved the book. So did the people in four other publishing houses, who wanted it badly enough to push up the price. For two days, the bids went back and forth and the price climbed higher and higher. Finally, the price went over a million dollars.

While Howard's company bid up the book, he had been constantly revising the profit-and-loss statements to reflect the ever-increasing advance. Toward the end of the second day, he began to think they'd have to pull out. He called a meeting of his key associates in the conference room.

"I don't want to let this book go," he said, "but the numbers are too tough." He passed around copies of the latest P&L.

Then Ben, the editorial director, made a suggestion. Ben had been a top editor at three publishing houses and had more experience than anyone else at the company. He had also been the first person Howard had hired after landing the top job. Ben picked up the P&L statement and suggested, "Throw this piece of paper out."

Ben pointed out that the numbers were meaningless. "We've been flying blind since yesterday afternoon," he said. "This is all about the collective instinct and wisdom of this group. I believe that this book will be a huge seller. We all do. And none of us think that this is a one-book author. We can't afford to lose the book, so here's what I suggest. We bump up our last offer by two hundred thousand and knock out the competition. And we add a clause giving a five-hundred-thousand floor with ten percent topping on the author's next book."

After clearing the offer with the chairman, Howard made the bid. His company won the book, and it was the year's biggest seller. Their bid also made it possible for them to buy the author's next book, which had even higher sales.

Workmen often use their thumb to make rough measurements. The more experienced the worker, the more likely that the rule of thumb was as good as the inches carefully marked out on a strip of wood. Just as there's nothing mystical about the ability to gauge length with a thumb, there's nothing otherworldly about what people call instinct. They can't explain the source of their conviction, because it doesn't come from one thing—it comes from years of experience about how best to do their job. Howard, surrounded by editors who had spent years learning their craft, decided to follow their instincts—and his own. The outcome taught him that the thumb can be a pretty good ruler.

Alexandra had a similar experience when she was editing a major magazine. The cover she had chosen for a particular issue was questioned by the business side. "Too controversial," they said. And they sent the cover out to a firm that conducted focus groups. The focus groups did not weigh in with Alexandra. Still, she passionately believed that the cover was right.

Because she refused to give in, the decision was kicked up to the company's chairman. "You're the only one who wants to run this cover," he said to her. "Our advertising department is against it. The testing hasn't been good. Why are you so positive it will work?"

"I've been in this business for a long time," Alexandra said. "Sometimes you just have a gut instinct and you have to go with it. Mine says that this is the cover we should run, that it's going to work."

The chairman decided to follow Alexandra's feeling. The issue jumped off the newsstand and provided a major boost to the magazine's circulation. "Thumbs Can Be Pretty Good Rulers"—but only when experience has taught you the length of your thumb. Until you have that experience, the only thing a thumb is good for is hitchhiking.

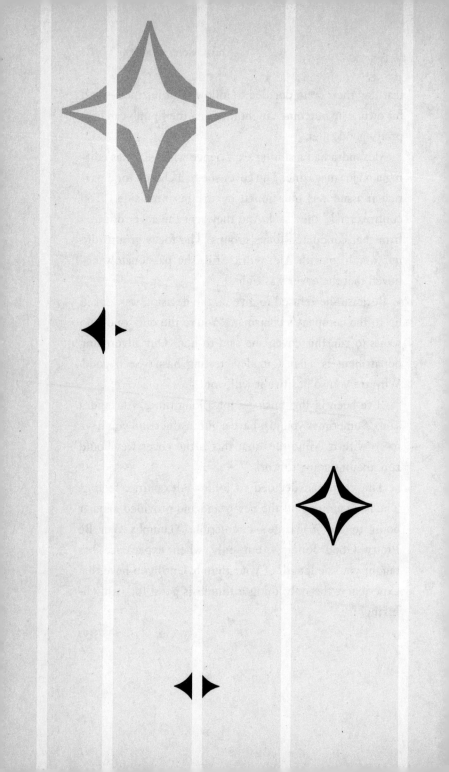

THE BUDDY TRAP

Over drinks, Miranda was talking about her first job, and how it almost ruined her career. Miranda's a screenwriter, and she and a young woman named Juliet started work at the movie studio on the same day. Both had studied film-making and saw their minor jobs as the first step toward major fame. Each day, they would meet for lunch in the cafeteria and, over containers of low-fat yogurt, talk about script ideas. They cast their imaginary films with unknown actors or actresses whose talents, they felt, were being neglected, and, convinced that success was just a meeting away, they wondered how they could wangle invitations to events where they might really get to know the people they passed in the halls.

But in actual fact, most nights Juliet hit the clubs and Miranda stayed home alone, working on her scripts. The pair were best buddies until the day Miranda showed up at lunch bursting to tell Juliet her news: the studio had optioned one of her scripts.

Miranda paused at this point in her story—she was, after all, a screenwriter, and she knew how to achieve dramatic effect. But we already knew that this story, like so many current movies, was about to have a predictable ending.

And it did, as Juliet insisted that she was the one who had suggested the idea on which Miranda had based her script; credit and money, Juliet said, should be shared. Miranda knew very well that the idea was her own, but since she couldn't prove it, she gave in.

"The studio decided not to make the movie," said Miranda. "I should have been depressed when they didn't exercise their option, but I was actually relieved. If they had, I could see myself tied to Juliet forever, the studio seeing us as a team, with me carrying her along for the rest of my life.

"I liked her. She was fun and she wanted the same sort of future I did. But I worked hard for it, and Juliet just dreamed. Not long after, I managed to get a job with another film company, and since I didn't pursue the friendship with Juliet it gradually faded away. Now I have a lot of co-workers I like. But after that experience I've steered clear of what I call 'The Buddy Trap.' Maybe having a best friend at work would be okay if you were each pursuing a different career path. But my experience taught me that there can be a danger zone and that friends better know where it is."

What interested us about Miranda's story was that you hear a lot of warnings about the dangers of office romance, but people rarely warn you about "The Buddy Trap." Miranda's not the only one who got caught. Patrick, a friend of Howard's, was named to head the division where he and his best friend both worked. Patrick was so fearful of showing favoritism that when a job opened up that by rights his old friend should have had, Patrick gave it to someone else instead. His friend quit both the job and the friendship.

Being friends with the people you work with is important, though obviously you will like some better than others. Even having a best friend at the office is okay, as long as you respect each other's careers. And as long as you don't make that friendship into a club that refuses admission to everyone else.

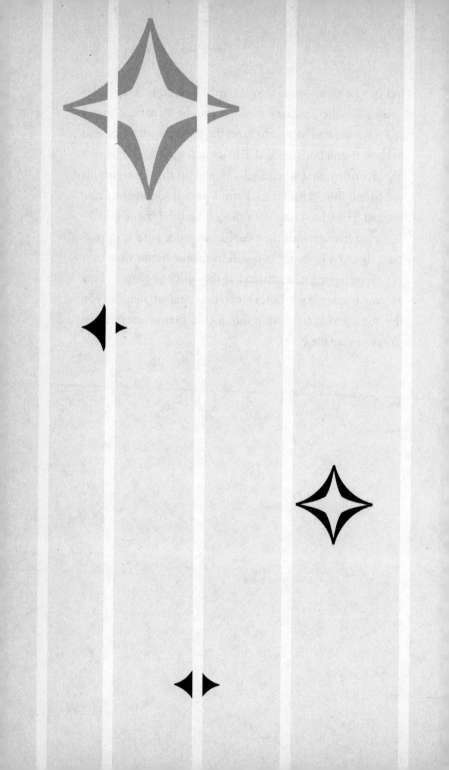

KID GLOVES ARE FOR
SPECIAL OCCASIONS

Luke is a financial planner—not an easy job in the recent economic climate. His company had recently—and oh so politely—suggested to several of the staff that they might be happier in other careers. The extra work had fallen on Luke, and when we ran into him at a friend's cocktail party, the strain was beginning to show.

His complaints led Howard to make what seemed a reasonable suggestion—dump a few of the extra accounts on someone else. We were surprised at Luke's instant rejection of the idea. It wasn't so much what Luke said that got our attention as the whispery way he said it, as though he were afraid someone might be listening.

It was none of our business, so we let it go, but several weeks later, Alexandra was trying to hail a cab when she realized that the man standing a few feet away, madly waving his arm at any vehicle with a yellow light, was Luke. The two agreed the taxi situation was hopeless and decided to sit out the five o'clock rush over coffee in a nearby hotel.

When Luke again complained of being overworked, Alexandra asked why he'd been so quick to reject Howard's suggestion that he share the load. "Because the only person I could share it with is Donald." Luke paused. "Donald is difficult."

"Difficult? How?" Alexandra asked.

"It's hard to explain," said Luke. "When you try to get Donald to do what he doesn't want to do, he becomes a sort of… presence. It's not quite a sulk, but he makes it clear he's not happy. Things get slammed around. He doesn't talk to you, or he becomes very curt. I mean, he does the job, but the atmosphere becomes very unpleasant. We all have learned to handle Donald with kid gloves."

"What you're saying," Alexandra countered, "is that Donald is a brat who intimidates people so he can get his own way."

Luke looked surprised. "I never thought of it that way. I guess I am a little afraid of the way Donald can ruin a good day."

"Which is why Donald gets away with it," Alexandra pointed out. "Kid gloves are only for special occasions, Luke. You may occasionally have to be cautious in the way you handle a colleague, but you shouldn't have to put on protection every day."

Luke muttered that it was kid gloves or boxing gloves, and Alexandra suggested he move the fight into another ring. "Go to your boss and ask him if he has any objection to your giving Donald some of the overload. Tell him you're working straight out and need a hand. Chances are he already thinks Donald is helping. Then put the accounts on Donald's desk with a note saying the boss suggested you to give them to him."

"He'll sulk," Luke said.

"Let him. Fight back by cheering him up. Whistle and sing happy songs. Buy him a chocolate bar and tell him it's to sweeten his bad mood. Keep doing nice, considerate things for him until he's ready to scream. Tell him, 'I hate to see you unhappy. I've made you my special project.' He'll find it easier to stop sulking than to have you buzzing around wearing your Happy Face."

Luke's change in attitude didn't make Donald a contender for the Mr. Congeniality prize, but at least he has stopped treating the rest of the office to his bad temper. Luke says the thing that did the trick was his insistence on giving Donald a neck massage to "relieve the tension that leads to bad temper."

Luke's position as a co-worker made it more difficult for him to take off the kid gloves, but many employers fail to deal with an employee's bad behavior. Good managers first make sure the behavior isn't due to a personal problem. Then they explain that prickly cacti live in deserts, where people can give them wide berth; in the closeness of an office, good manners rule, and tantrums and sulks will be shown the door.

MANAGING UP

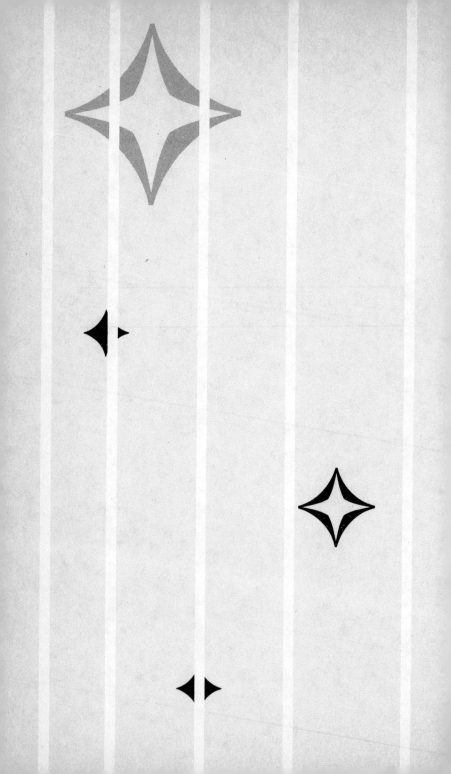

Jane learned these Magic Words on her first job, as an intern in the editorial department of a metropolitan paper. Jane was on the copy desk, working along with Adam, whose job it was to make sure that the experts had it right. When Adam came across a reference to a Renaissance painter which he was sure was in error, he didn't change the copy. Instead he beckoned Jane to follow him and headed for the library. Once he was certain of his facts, Adam took the article back to the critic and pointed out where it was wrong. The critic disagreed. He was the expert, not Adam. Adam suggested that the critic come up with a source. The critic pulled a book from a pile on his desk, looked up the name, and, greatly embarrassed, admitted he was wrong.

"Never confront a know-it-all until you've made sure that you know more," Adam told Jane. "I'll do this kind of thing four or five times with each writer—let them insist they're right after I've made sure they're wrong. After they've been embarrassed a few times, they take my word for things. Once I've established my authority, the egos are easier to deal with."

The critic had gone into battle armed to the teeth. He was no match for Adam, who, knowing his opponent, was armed to the ears.

It's not enough to know as much as the competition. You have to know a little bit more. Fred owns a business that specializes in antique textiles. He not only sells them, he repairs them. "Providing that service for customers gives me an edge in the market," he says, but adds that that's only part of what makes his firm so successful. "When you do hands-on work with things, you learn about them differently. You see why a piece was shaped in a certain way, what was possible and what was not. You learn what different fibers can do. You begin to think like the creator, not the connoisseur. I'd say that most of the people in my business are pretty knowledgeable about textiles. But they're book-knowledgeable and eye-knowledgeable. I've got all that, but I've also got a knowledge that comes only through the hands. It's that extra thing that makes a difference."

There is another reason why it pays to be armed to the ears. Most jobs involve contacts outside your own field. If you're a salesman, you also have dealings with the service and accounting departments. Before you get on the phone and roar that the account must be straightened out "NOW!" or that the part better be there by 3 P.M., you have to know whether either thing is possible. Having a successful career involves knowing whether someone is being honest or simply uncooperative when he or she responds to your request by saying, "It can't be done."

As an editor, Alexandra needed to understand the capabilities of the company that printed the magazine before she insisted they rush a job through. It was important for her to know what the process involved and how fast it could be done. Most of us, whatever our professions, need to know not only our own job, but the work done by those who support us. Then, when a request is met by "It can't be done," we have the satisfaction of countering that stonewall response by saying it *can* be done and politely explaining how.

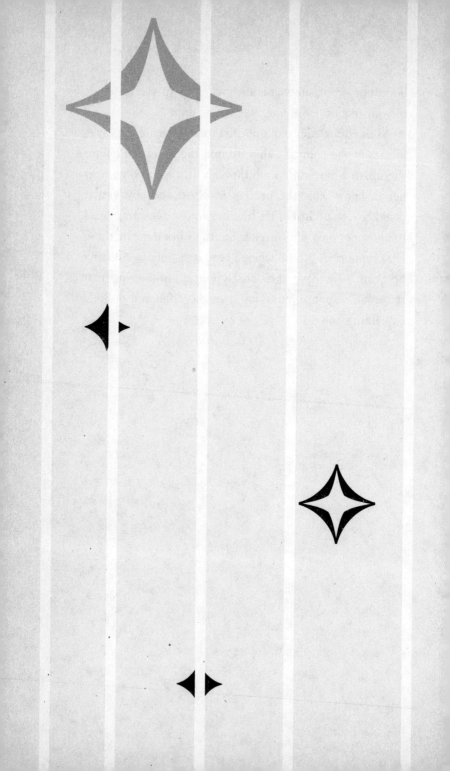

"WRONG" IS THE RIGHT WORD
IN THE RIGHT PLACE

Warren finally landed his dream job, number two in the media-buying division of a large advertising agency in San Francisco. His boss, Mario, was an open and imaginative executive who had met Warren at a trade show and quickly offered him a job.

Every Monday, Mario held a staff meeting to review the upcoming week's agenda. He ran the meeting efficiently, so that everyone got a chance to speak but if anyone strayed too far from the subject under discussion, Mario reeled him back in. At the end of each meeting, Mario would take a minute to tell the staff his ideas for upcoming projects. This would be followed by an open discussion, with everyone throwing out suggestions on how to implement or modify them. Although the discussions could get spirited, no one ever found fault with any of Mario's proposals. After all, Mario was the boss. Warren, witnessing the caution shown by the rest of the staff, suspected that, though he encouraged open debate, Mario didn't brook criticism.

After Warren had been at the firm for six months, Mario ended one of the staff meetings with the suggestion that they open a satellite office in San Diego. The idea was a bad one, doomed to fail, not only because the proposed budget was too small but because Mario was proposing to syphon off staff from the main office to get it going. The main office was shorthanded as it was.

After Mario made his presentation, he asked the rest of the staff to comment.

A muffled chorus of "sounds interesting," "could work" filled the air.

Then, in a not-so-muffled voice, Warren spoke up. "Mario, I think it's a lousy idea." And he explained his objections, cogently and in great detail.

When he finished, no one else spoke. Finally, Mario nodded his head and acknowledged the argument: "Very interesting." The meeting broke up at that, and Warren headed back to his office. His uneasiness about Mario's response grew when his secretary buzzed him and said that Mario wanted to see him right away.

"Sit down," Mario said as Warren came into his office.

"Is there a problem?" Warren asked.

"Yes and no," said Mario, fiddling with a pencil. "Let me start with 'no.' I have no problem with your speaking your mind, Warren. That's why I hired you. And I admit it—you're absolutely right about the San Diego office; it's a bad idea. I thank you for an excellent analysis. Now for the 'yes.' "

Here it comes, thought Warren.

"In the future, I'd appreciate it if you gave me those types of thoughts in private. It's not just because I'm thin-skinned, though, unfortunately, I am. It's just that I don't want to start a 'Let's critique the boss' club here. Do you understand?"

Warren did understand, and he learned his lesson. In any office there's a fine line between being a yes-man and choosing not to embarrass the boss by criticizing him in front of other employees. In the future, when Mario voiced a bad idea while others were around, Warren kept his mouth shut. Later, in a private meeting or in a memo, he offered his dissenting position. "Wrong Is the Right Word." But be careful you don't say it in the wrong place.

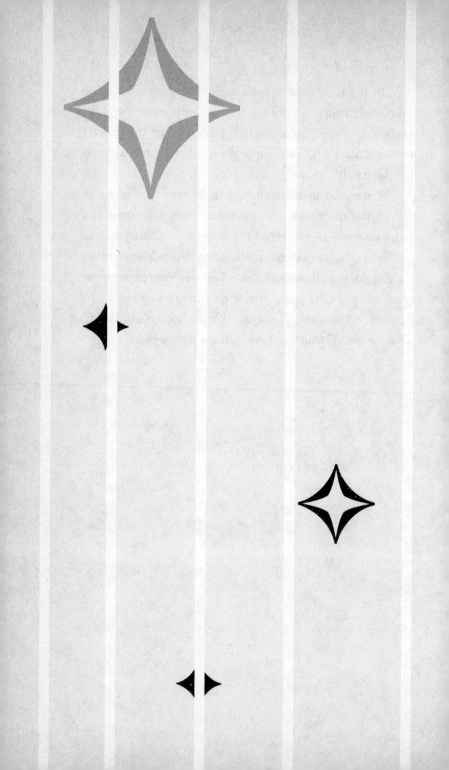

What child doesn't love the teeter-totter, soaring up into the air, and then softly drifting down? Of course, it demands a child on each end, one acting as counterweight to the other. If the child on the bottom climbs off, the child on the top, instead of floating down, crashes to the ground.

It was the realization that a teeter-totter is a game that takes two that made Howard think of these Magic Words. They were inspired by his friend Audrey, an account executive with a large public-relations firm, who told him about her problems on the job.

"It's not that I don't like to compete," Audrey said. "Honestly, I do. I've run in seven marathons and played volleyball in college. But the man I work for, Jerry, is constantly pitting me against another man in the office. One day Jerry thinks I'm the best and is pushing at Matt to improve. The next week it's Matt who can do no wrong. I never know from day to day whether I'm going to be up or down."

Audrey told Howard that in the beginning she had liked

Matt. They'd lunched together occasionally, exchanged favorite novels. "We're both fans of Michael Crichton and Patricia Cornwell," said Audrey. Matt reviewed proposals Audrey had written, and she did the same for him. "I thought of him as a friend as well as a colleague," said Audrey. "Then the company hired a new CEO."

Somewhere in his career, the new executive had picked up the idea of management based on what he called "creative tension." What this came down to was pitting the staff against one another. "Within weeks," said Audrey, "Matt and I had become competitors. In the past, before the new CEO took over, either we'd be given a presentation to work on alone, or, occasionally, it would be a joint assignment. The new man's policy was to assign us both the same project and choose the one he felt was best. And he didn't do the choosing in private. At the weekly meetings devoted to new business, he'd hold them both up and say what was wrong with one and what was right about the other. Each week one of us got put in the hot seat, made to feel inadequate and humiliated.

"I had decided to talk to Matt, but he beat me to the punch, suggesting that we meet away from the office over dinner. 'I think we have to get together,' he said. 'Let's say Artie's Pub at seven. Be prepared to consume a few Mojitos.' "

That night, for the first time since the CEO had set them at each other mano a mano, the two were able to laugh about the situation. "The Mojitos helped," Audrey admitted, laughing. "But we realized that, by going along with it, we made the competition possible. We were constantly on a teeter-totter, one up and one down. It was terrible for us, and it was a waste of our time where the company was concerned. Of course, we couldn't say that to the CEO. We decided that we couldn't change his management style, and that, if he wanted to pay us for wasting our time, that was his business. But we could at least spare ourselves humiliation. In the future, we worked on both proposals jointly. One would have Matt's name, one would have mine, but we both knew that they were ours. Gradually, so did others in the company.

"You might think, with other people knowing, the CEO would have found out what we were doing. But Matt and I suspected that a man who was into humiliating his employees wasn't going to be listening to office gossip. He never did pick up on it.

"That was an extreme case of what Matt and I took to calling 'The Teeter-Totter Effect,' but I've encountered it less seriously since. Now, since I know that it takes two to make the teeter-totter go up or go down, I find a way to slide off my end."

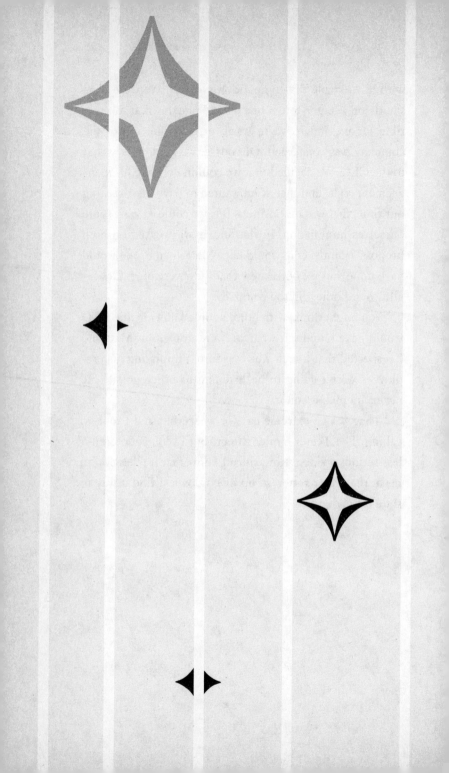

"No one is under more intense scrutiny than the person who is being deliberately ignored," said Christina, who is product manager of a firm that makes cosmetics. "Until our president retired, his best friend in the company was the man I worked under. Arthur was the vice-president for sales and marketing, and he and the president played golf together, socialized together, went to all the right charity functions. Since he was under the president's wing, no one in the company would have dared to insinuate that Arthur was inept. But he was. The rest of us covered up all the mistakes he made while Arthur spent hours making the office rounds, taking up everyone's time. Not good, because, in addition to our own work, we were always extra busy fixing the things he'd gotten wrong. No question. Arthur was a burden.

"When the new president took over, he wasn't interested in Arthur's golf score. He wanted to know what Arthur was doing for the company. It took him about a week to figure it out. Nothing."

Office gossip being what it is, everyone knew when the president called Arthur in for a long meeting. Office bets were that Arthur was being given a chance to save face, to resign. But the expected announcement didn't come. Although people in the know said that the president had told Arthur he wanted him out, Arthur had resisted. Perhaps he had asked for time to find another job. All anyone really knew was that Arthur had hunkered down.

After a month, the new management turned Arthur into a nonperson. When retail chains were coming, Arthur wasn't informed. When product meetings were scheduled, Arthur was sent out on some meaningless assignment and his assistant was asked to attend. There was nothing on Arthur's desk but the *Wall Street Journal*. Arthur was being shunned. When he gave someone on his staff an assignment, it was instantly countermanded from above.

The way the new management saw it, Arthur wasn't playing by the rules. He should have resigned and let them bring in one of their own people. Among the older staff, opinion was that Arthur was holding out for more severance—a bit more gold on the parachute and he'd agree to bail out. For whatever reason, Arthur remained, and the atmosphere in the office grew more tense daily. The staff knew that when giants are fighting on the field, small folks who get in the way can get crushed.

It may have looked as though Arthur was being ignored, but the president had his radar right on him, tracking every move he made. "None of us wanted to lose our jobs because we'd accidentally shown up as blips on the screen," said

Christina. "It wasn't a time to take sides or to become too visible by suggesting new ideas. It was a time to fly low and keep out of sight." Christina said she and the rest of the staff had Magic Words they used during the days when the president and Arthur were fighting it out: "Make like a Prairie Dog."

"Arthur finally left," she said, "but those six months when the big guys battled it out were the worst I've ever had in this business."

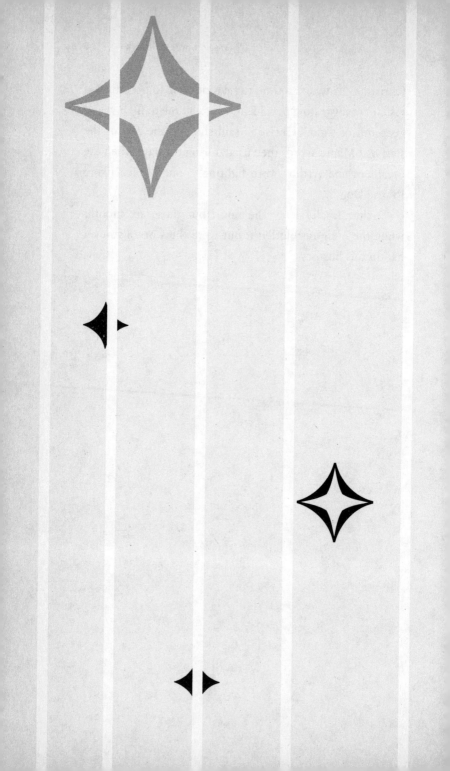

THE PAUSE BUTTON

Alexandra's first boss was a smart, warm, and energetic man named Victor. He knew every aspect of his job running a large consumer magazine, and the job of everyone who worked for him. But a week or so after she started, Alexandra overheard one of her colleagues refer to him as Vic Vacillation, and it didn't take her long to figure out why.

"Alexandra," he said, "I love your story idea on plastic surgery in Japan. Let's put Gina on it and try to get it in the March issue."

Alexandra hurried back to her office, got the freelancer on the phone, and explained the project. She then called the travel department to arrange for plane tickets to Tokyo and a hotel room. Finally, Alexandra called the managing editor to let her know that Vic had ordered the piece for the March issue and that something else would have to be pulled.

Two days later, Victor called Alexandra into his office.

"I'm having second thoughts about that plastic-surgery piece," he said.

"Why, Vic? It's a natural."

"Do our readers really care about what they're doing in Japan? It's not as though these new techniques are available in the United States. At least not yet. It's an interesting idea, but maybe we ought to sit on it for a while."

Once more Alexandra hurried back to her office, this time to call Gina, who, luckily, had not yet left for the airport. Then there was the apologetic call to the travel department, which had to cancel the arrangements. Vic's vacillations had wasted her afternoon.

His stop-go-and-stop problem ranged from canceling lunch engagements to changing the magazine cover five or six times each issue. Alexandra was beginning to have doubts about her ability to cope. When she confided her uneasiness to her old college roommate, Jan suggested Alexandra unwind with her over dinner. Jan was staying with her rich and elderly great-aunt in a large and rambling apartment on Central Park West. Aunt Carrie had prepared a simple but excellent meal, and as they ate, she told charming stories of her travels in India. Jan had gotten a video for them to watch, and after dinner the three settled down on the couch. The minute Jan started the movie, Aunt Carrie jumped up and announced that she would get cookies from the kitchen. Jan stopped the movie until Aunt Carrie returned. This time, as the movie began, Aunt Carrie jumped up and said that perhaps she should have gotten them cake. She once again disappeared. When this happened a third time, Alexandra sympathized with Jan.

"It's okay. I just hit pause. In the family, Aunt Carrie's famous for changing her mind. When remote controls came out, my brother grabbed it and said, 'Look. You can make it pause. Whoever invented it must have had an Aunt Carrie.' "

That evening with Jan and her aunt solved Alexandra's problem with Vic Vacillation. The next time he did stop, go, and stop, Alexandra hit the pause button. She didn't do what he'd told her to do. She waited several hours or days, depending on the situation, and then stopped in his office and pushed him to change his mind.

"I was thinking about that survey on shopping you suggested. Do you really think it's worth it? Getting a company to do it will cost a bundle."

"You know, I've been thinking the same thing. Let's put it on hold."

For as long as she worked for the magazine, Alexandra regularly subjected Vic's plans to delay and discouragement. If he persisted, she went ahead. Since that long-ago job, Alexandra has come across other people who subscribe to Vic's management practice of stop, go, and stop—and she always counters them by pressing the pause button.

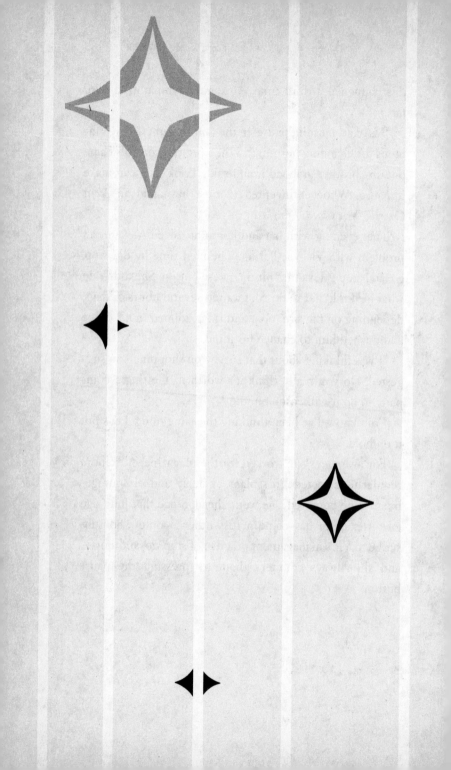

RAISING YOUR VOICE CAN WORK
BETTER THAN RAISING YOUR HAND

Alexandra has a friend who is a wimp. She is so worried about being pushy that she frequently stands outside an empty ladies' room because her gingerly attempt to open the door has met with resistance. As she waits patiently, a not-so-patient line forms behind her. Invariably, after three or four minutes, someone stomps up to the head of the line and gives the door handle a shake and a turn, in an attempt to force the occupant to exit. The door opens. There is no occupant, just a door that sticks. Alexandra's friend is embarrassed once again. You'd think she'd learn, but this is a scenario she has repeated many times. Her mother's admonition that good girls wait their turn still has her in its grip, and it has definitely hurt her at work.

It is not just women who suffer professionally because they are afraid of appearing too aggressive. Many men also hesitate to push their way into the spotlight. They'll submit memos regarding their ideas, but don't ask them to speak up at meetings. In large groups you'll find them raising a tentative hand, asking for a chance to speak. It never comes, because the chair's attention is claimed by the more aggressive people who have leapt to their feet.

In an era when people vie to appear on TV, happy to confess to unspeakable crimes as long as it gains them a minute in the spotlight, the retiring person seems an anachronism, playing by rules that others no longer follow. We're all for good manners, and career success does not rest on being pushy, but most of us have something to say, and it pays professionally to learn how to get people's attention before we say it.

There are coaches who can teach you how to pitch your voice so that you are able to control the room. They train you to speak without the hesitant throat-clearing and "hummm"s that stall a presentation. If you have serious trouble talking out at meetings, hire one to help you.

Have something specific to say and, once you've said it, sit down. It's easy to weaken a strong presentation by not knowing how to end it. Think of yourself as an actor. When you finish your scene, get off the stage.

The final trick behind learning how to raise your voice instead of raising your hand is confidence, and that comes from being well prepared in your job. When you understand what your company does and have ideas about how it can do things better, you'll have the motivation you need to speak up instead of shutting down.

IF YOU WANT TO WOO
A TURKEY BUZZARD, YOU HAVE TO
PLAY HER GAME

Howard came up with these Magic Words when Alexandra told him about her friend Sally, who was trying to get a certain company to carry her line of women's sports clothes. "Sally knew that the head of the company, a man named McIntyre, would love her stuff," said Alexandra, "but she hadn't been able to get through to him. Whenever she called his office, his secretary would chant, 'Mr. McIntyre is out of town.' Sally had gone to endless cocktail parties because friends had mentioned that McIntyre was also invited. He was always a no-show. When I said that Sally was ready to give up, Howard grinned and said, 'Turkey buzzard.'

"It's an old joke," Howard explained, "about an oversexed rooster who's had his way with every hen in the barnyard. He's even gone after the ducks and the geese. The farmer notices how thin the rooster is and warns him, 'If you don't take it easy, you're going to kill yourself.' Sure enough, the next day the farmer goes out to the barnyard and finds the rooster stretched out on the ground, a turkey buzzard flying in tight circles overhead. 'I warned you,' the farmer says sadly. Whereupon the rooster opens one eye. 'Shhhhh! If you want to woo a turkey buzzard, you have to play her game.' "

A couple of nights later, Alexandra was at the opera and who should be standing next to her in the lobby during intermission but Sally. "I told her Howard's story, and we both laughed," Alexandra said. "If I thought anything, it was that Sally may not have gotten the contract but at least she came away with a joke.

"I didn't see Sally for a couple of months," Alexandra went on. "Then, one day, we found ourselves standing in line together at the fish market. Sally told me that when she stopped laughing about the turkey buzzard she started giving some serious thought to the moral of the story. What was McIntyre's game? It certainly wasn't cocktail parties."

Sally did some digging. She called a few mutual friends, and one of them told her that McIntyre was obsessed with shooting, that his hobby was skeet shooting. He belonged to a club outside the city and spent almost every weekend out there, competing with other club members. Sally knew that she wouldn't get a hearing from McIntyre if she turned up not knowing the difference between the stock and the barrel. If she was going to play his game, she had to play it well, so she bought a shotgun and hired an instructor. After a month of intense practice (and a bottle of arnica to soothe her sore shoulder), Sally felt she was ready to join the club. Three months after she first stood next to McIntyre, waiting for the high-house clay bird to be thrown into the air, she had a contract, a new hobby, and, at his suggestion, an addition to her line: vests, jackets, and gloves for women who shoot. And we had learned new Magic Words, which remind us that if you want to make a successful business connection, it pays to find out whom you're dealing with.

✧

Though not all of us participated in team sports while growing up, we've all been taught to be team players. Certainly, it's not much of a stretch to think of you and your co-workers as a team. You probably spend as much time with these teammates as you do with family and friends. Which makes it extremely difficult to blow the whistle on someone you know and perhaps like a lot.

"Whistle Softly" are Sandi's Magic Words, and she came up with them well before the scandals over Enron and the like tarnished the image of corporate America. An account supervisor at a large insurance company, she discovered that a colleague in her division was cooking the books. "I knew I had to do something, but I didn't know what," she said. "I kept thinking of all the names we used to shout at each other in grade school—'snitch,' 'squealer,' 'rat,' 'tattletale.' That last was the worst. I didn't want to be a tattletale. It meant you'd turned in your friends."

Sandi had discovered, quite by chance, that a woman in

the division had been boosting revenues by booking policies at rates that were higher than the actual premiums. Although Gloria didn't actually skim the money, by jumping up the payments she made it look as though her section was selling more than others. And when bonus time came around, Gloria got top dollar.

"Obviously, Gloria liked getting a big bonus," said Sandi, "but I think the real reason she did it was for the praise. All the higher-ups thought Gloria was a star. They'd drop by her desk to tell her how well she was doing."

For two weeks Sandi tried to decide what to do. "At first I told myself that I wanted no part of it. Let someone else catch her. I'm a manager, not a detective. Gradually, I admitted to myself that what Gloria was doing put us all in jeopardy. If it went on, the fraud could materially affect the company. Her division, and maybe even mine, could be closed down. People might be out of work. So I decided to confront her. I invited her for lunch and told her I was aware of what she was doing. At first she denied it and accused me of being jealous of her success. Finally, she backed down and admitted it. But she said it was only a temporary situation and that she was trying to straighten it out. She asked me to give her a few weeks. Reluctantly, I agreed.

"The few weeks turned into two months. Every time I'd approach her, she'd beg for 'just a little more time.' I was beginning to feel like her accomplice. I knew I could go to the COO, but people would see me as a turncoat."

Sandi realized, as do we, that whistle-blowing is a heroic act and being a hero is never easy. If the scandal is big enough, the media will make a brief fuss over the whistle-blower before moving on to the next day's news. Once the media attention dwindles, the company may isolate the whistle-blower, making it hard to stay on. It's an old tradition, shooting the messenger who brings bad news. Other organizations rarely rush to hire such a person. Who wants a watchdog barking in the hall? And there is another consideration: you may be about to report the corruption to a higher-up who's in on the deal.

So what do you do? Sandi's procedure of first confronting the criminal was the best way to begin; if you're lucky, that will put an end to it. Since Gloria's delaying tactics simply prolonged the fraud, Sandi had to find another way to stop it. She didn't want to go public by reporting to the COO, so she decided to blow the whistle, but softly, in a way that wouldn't make her look like a snitch. In a meeting of her division, Sandi stood up and in injured innocence asked, "Why didn't you tell all the divisions you were raising the rates? It doesn't seem fair that you gave Gloria's a head start."

Needless to say, the tactic was effective. Gloria lost her job. The scandal was averted.

We like the way Sandi got awkward information out into the open, but we've seen other people use other methods, such as writing an anonymous memo, or making the information available to a media contact who could bring it to light without revealing the source. When you decide to become a whistle-blower, whistle softly, but know that sometimes, when the issue is serious enough, you may have to pucker your lips, blow, and face the fallout.

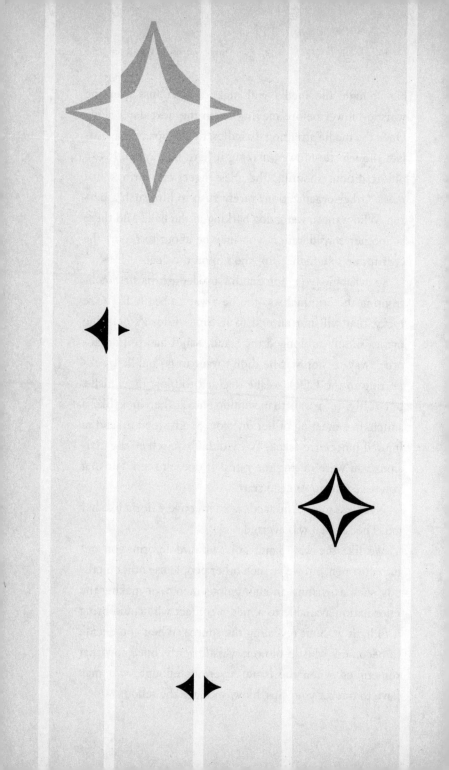

Asking for something can be difficult, whether it's a small favor, such as borrowing a neighbor's lawnmower, or a big one, like asking a friend for a loan. But asking for a raise is not asking for a favor; it's asking for something you've earned. People who sit around waiting to be paid more money are missing the point. Requesting a raise should be part of your job, and you should prepare for the annual "I'd like more money" meeting with the same care you use putting together a report. Over the years, both of us have been through the process many times. Through trial and error, we've developed some techniques that work.

THE DONE LIST: Never ask for a raise without carefully preparing a list of the things you've done over the past year. Have you saved the company money? Have you brought in new business? Have you suggested changes that result in more efficient management? Did someone's quitting force you to take on two jobs? Or have you helped the company attract new talent? Alexandra once knew a woman who put her vacation house on the market for much more than it was worth. When questioned about the high price tag, she said, "Well, it may not be what it's worth, but it's what I need." This is *not* an attitude that will win you a raise. Do not tell your boss that you need more money because you have two children at college. Tell him what you're worth, not what you need.

TIMING IS ALL: Do the asking, don't wait to be called in and handed a sack of gold. About three months before it's time for the annual raise, make an appointment with your boss to tell him why you think you've earned one. Explain that you don't expect it to take effect until the year is up, but that you'd like to give him or her time to consider your request. Don't, however, ask for a raise after a lousy third quarter, in the midst of a company scandal, when there are rumors of a takeover, or when someone new has just taken over your division. Do put a bid in when the company is doing well, or—though it is very bad policy to allude to this directly—if the CEO's extravagant lifestyle has recently been profiled in a major magazine. It is all right to mention the current rate of inflation, though it probably won't do any good.

THE TRADING SEASON: Sometimes your company will not be in a position to give you a raise and the answer will be no. Be prepared to hear that the cupboard is bare, and come prepared to trade. Have a list of possible perks that could be offered in lieu of money. Roger knew that sales were off and that his company was unlikely to come up with a raise. But the slack sales also meant that there was less work. Roger prepared what he called the "bargaining box." It contained a variety of perks that would serve in place of money. His first suggestion, that he work a four-day week until business picked up, was rejected. His second proposal, that he be given an extra three weeks' vacation in lieu of the raise, was accepted. Barbara's trade was to give up the raise in favor of a larger end-of-the-year bonus. She says that next year, if the company's performance continues to falter, she's going to ask for a better title, mentioned in the past but never given. If your company is publicly traded (and if business is bad, the price is probably low), you might settle for stock options. Or the larger office sitting empty two doors down from yours. Someone who's had to plead that money is in short supply may be particularly susceptible to your list of compensations that won't cost cash.

SOME DON'TS: Don't say that since someone else in the office is making more you're entitled to the same. Don't threaten to quit unless you really plan to do so. Don't use the offer of another job as a lever unless you're prepared to take it. Don't give up. Sometimes the answer is a flat-out no: no money, no perks. Say that you understand the timing is bad but you'd like to discuss the subject again in three months. If repeated requests are turned down—and the company isn't about to go belly-up—see our entry on "Scarlet Signs." You may be getting a message you shouldn't ignore.

MANAGING DOWN

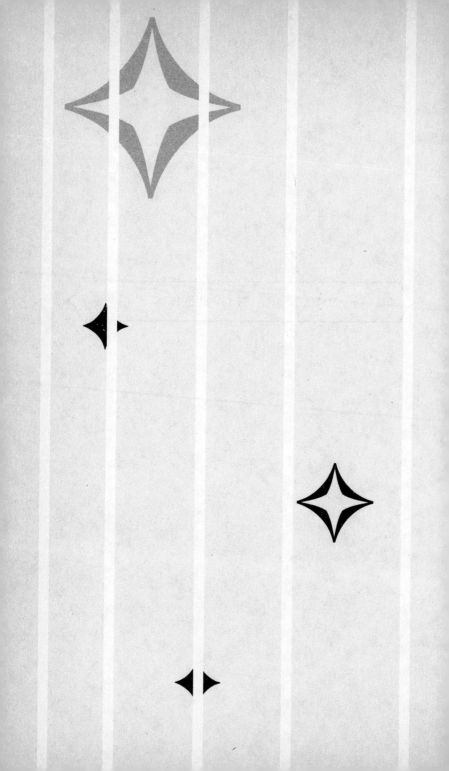

We got these magic words from Dennis, an old friend. He uses them all the time and says they always work, both in and out of the office. Dennis, the managing partner in a large architectural firm, says he picked up this very useful phrase years ago, from his first boss.

"Arnie hired me right out of school to work for his company, a mid-sized architectural firm in San Diego that specialized in small office buildings, shopping centers, school additions—mostly commercial work, though they did do some residences. The first big assignment he gave me was a seven-thousand-seat basketball arena at a college just north of L.A. We had beaten out three other firms for the job. The rest of the team consisted of two senior partners and two other young architects who had a couple of years more experience than I had. My particular assignment was making sure that our plans conformed to all the various city and state codes. That ranged from stairs to fire exits, restrooms to electrical power. It wasn't the Frank Lloyd

Wright stuff I'd dreamed of, but the excitement of actually working as an architect was pretty heady stuff.

"The group would meet twice a week with Arnie to go over their progress. The two senior partners took turns chairing the meeting, and most of the time Arnie just sat and listened. Right from the start, they began to fall behind schedule. There were a number of small things that delayed them, but they weren't the real problem. The major tie-up was the design of the roof. It looked sensational, but it had only been used once before, in the construction of an ice-skating arena in Finland. The roof needed a special type of lightweight steel girder that was made of overlapping plates of titanium. Finding the right steel mill to produce the girders to the specs was proving to be a nightmare. Also, costs for it were running forty percent over their estimates.

"At one of our meetings, Arnie suddenly spoke up. 'Get out the tweezers.'

"None of us had any idea what he was talking about. We just sat there, waiting for him to continue.

" 'The tweezer is a beautiful little instrument, and it's designed for a single use: to remove one splinter, or one hair, or one of anything. We have here a problem that calls out for a tweezer.'

"Arnie went on to explain that the overall concept for the arena was fine. That's why we had won out over the other firms. But the roof had become a problem, and the roof was not the reason we'd gotten the job. Arnie sketched out an alternative roofing system, which would cost a lot less, and pointed out, 'We just need the tweezers to remove the one, and only, problem we have.'

"I'm thankful to Arnie," Dennis told us. "For giving me my set of tweezers and showing me how to use them. Most problems do not require wholesale changes. You need to isolate what's really wrong, not blow up the whole thing. Then you get out the tweezers and remove the splinter."

For a while after hearing Dennis's story, we drove each other crazy with these Magic Words. When Howard complained that the plans for his new kitchen looked wrong, Alexandra was there to remind him, "Get out the tweezers." When Alexandra decided she'd chosen the wrong photographs for an exhibit, it was Howard's turn to cut the problem down to size. When our friend Mac said that morale in his office had taken a dive, we asked him to isolate the cause, and he pinned the problem on Melancholy Mel, a fellow so pessimistic he'd put the entire office under a cloud. We told Mac to use the tweezers on Mel, and within a week, he'd been plucked out of the office and told that from then on he would be working at home. You don't cut off your finger when you get a splinter; you get out the tweezers and remove that tiny, troublesome piece of wood.

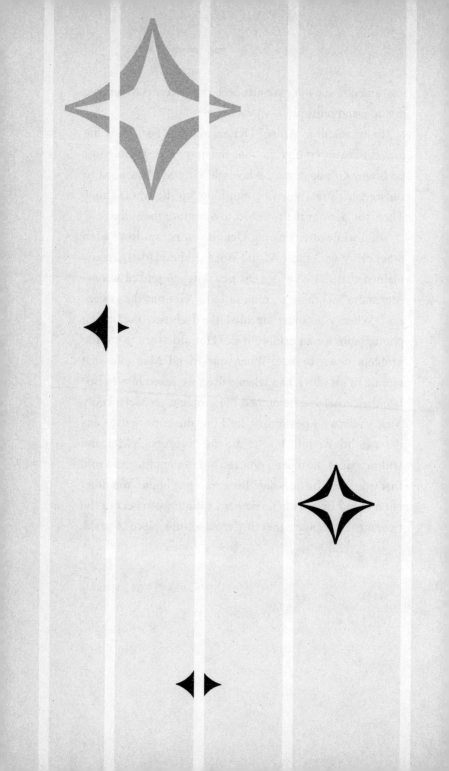

Howard's first experience with what he calls " 'I' strain" came years ago, when he watched the man he worked for sabotage a plan that would have improved sales. His boss had done it for the worst possible reason: he hadn't thought of it himself. Up to that point, Howard had considered Ted a good manager. After that, he began to notice that Ted treated employees well until they did something that threatened his ego. Ted's book of management was written in the blink of an "I," and he preferred that underlings linger on the lower rungs—of business and of life.

Ted's determination to be top dog sounds fairly harmless—even a bit silly—in terms of day-to-day business, but Howard began to see that Ted's need to be front and center kept him from following up on his staff's suggestions. Instead of behaving professionally, he adopted the view that success and good fortune were a zero-sum game, with life's prizes being finite. In Ted's worldview, someone else's accomplishments diminished his own.

His experience with Ted's left a lasting impression and inspired Howard's Magic Words "Up Close and Impersonal," a reminder that knowing how to keep the "I" out of it is an important management tool.

The business press has presented plenty of stories about CEOs who, if called upon to recite the vowels, would chant "A, E, I, I, I, I . . ." These self-centered souls can't survive unless they're surrounded by paid pals, heads nodding up and down in agreement, like dolls on a Chevy dashboard. Unfortunately, this means they rarely get a warning that someone better is pulling up behind. Now, we aren't so naïve as to think that the bad guys always lose, or that all executives who suffer from "I" strain get their comeuppance, but we do know that letting a little air out of the ego guarantees that you won't get stuck in quite so many tight places.

So—does managing up close and impersonal just mean keeping your ego out of the office, or does it also mean keeping out emotions? Everyone knows that a good boss cares about the problems of employees, right? Well, yes, up to a point, because there is a line a manager should not cross. A good employer gives time and support to people who are facing a serious illness, understands the occasional crises that face parents when child care fails, looks the other way when a personal situation temporarily cuts into an employee's productivity—but does not get overly involved.

Howard saw the importance of impersonal management when his friend Jed became so upset by an assistant's ordeal with a diabetic child that the work of the office suffered as a result. Jed read the literature, set staff members to surfing the Internet for the latest research, took his employee out to lunch several times a week to cheer her up. His obsession, kindhearted though it was, disrupted the office and caused resentment among other employees, who felt that their own problems were being ignored.

An effective manager gets the "I" out of it. Does someone without your experience have the audacity to have a good idea? Great. Use it. Does the ancient and irritating employee who has taken on the unofficial role of company historian come into your office muttering about how, once upon a time, they did things differently? And does that "differently" make a lot of sense? Go for it. Is someone in the middle of a difficult divorce? Cut the person some slack, but don't cruise in close and say, "I can help." Your job as a manager isn't to give in to emotions—whether they are good ones or bad. Your job is to be up close and impersonal.

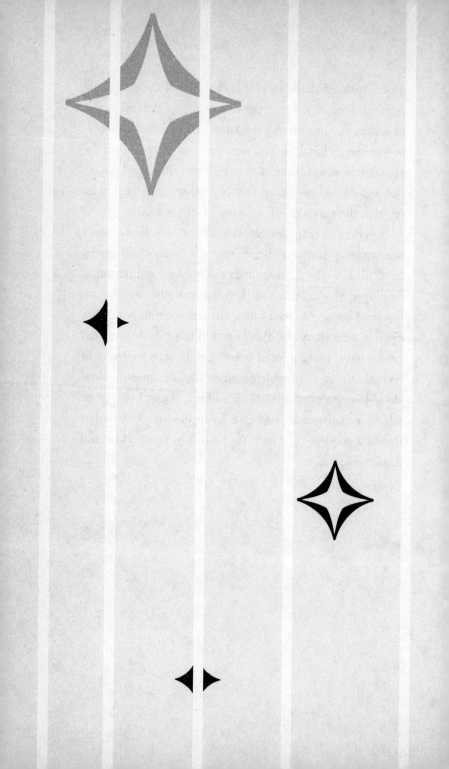

I'M GOING TO LEAD
BETWEEN THE LINES

When Ethan was a boy, his father worked at the local paper mill. A good union member, he taught Ethan the importance of overlooking the petty internal feuds that might divide the mill workers, and to concentrate on the importance of a united front. During high school and college, Ethan worked summers at the mill, helping to pay for his schooling. After graduation, he served several years in the army. His time in France and Germany satisfied whatever wanderlust he may have had, and he found himself longing for home.

When he came back to the mill, his job put him on the side of management, but his knowledge of the operation and the friendships he'd made earlier made him more an intermediary than an adversary when bargaining time came around. Eventually, Ethan was named to run the mill. His father, long since retired, took him to lunch to celebrate. He also gave him some advice: "When I was shop steward and some new regulation was proposed, I learned to look at it pretty carefully. The person who wrote it might mean one thing, but someone who came along later and had the job of enforcing it could see it differently. I learned to read between the lines. That's what you should do. Look at things from every angle. And don't only read between the lines. Lead between the lines. It's easy to believe you're boxed in. The union thinks management is trying to keep it in bounds. Management thinks the union is doing the same. So a good union leader—and a good manager—learns how to use the rules instead of being bound by them. First come up with a solution that fits the situation. Then, when you've got your solution, find a way to make it fit the rules."

"The first time I took my dad's advice," said Ethan, "was when I stupidly got myself in trouble with the union. I was working over the weekend, and one of our suppliers delivered a load of pallets. They could have stayed where he dumped them until Monday. They *should* have stayed there until Monday. But it was a nice day, and I decided I'd get the forklift and move them to where they belonged. You know, I was probably just sick of being in the office, and I wanted to get out in the yard and work outside, the way I used to. I finished, went back to my office, and suddenly realized what I'd done. I'm management and I'd done a union job. We were going to have to pay a union member for my moving those pallets.

"There's one of the drivers in the yard who's been a big pain in the neck. He's got what I call 'rule rage'—the tiniest infraction and he starts threatening a strike. I knew he'd be on my case first thing Monday, and, knowing him, he'd claim the money we were going to have to pay. I didn't want to give him more power than he already had. I thought about what my dad had said: find a solution, and then make it fit the rules. So before I went home I wrote out a check for another one of the operators, typed a memo saying why he was being paid, and taped the envelope to his locker.

"Come Monday, Rule Rage storms into my office. 'Who moved the pallets?' I confessed, and before he could say anything I added, 'I know I was wrong. I've already made out the check.' Rule Rage starts to smile. 'I gave it to Hal first thing this morning.' "

"I'm Going to Lead Between the Lines." Those are Magic Words whether you're a shop steward or management.

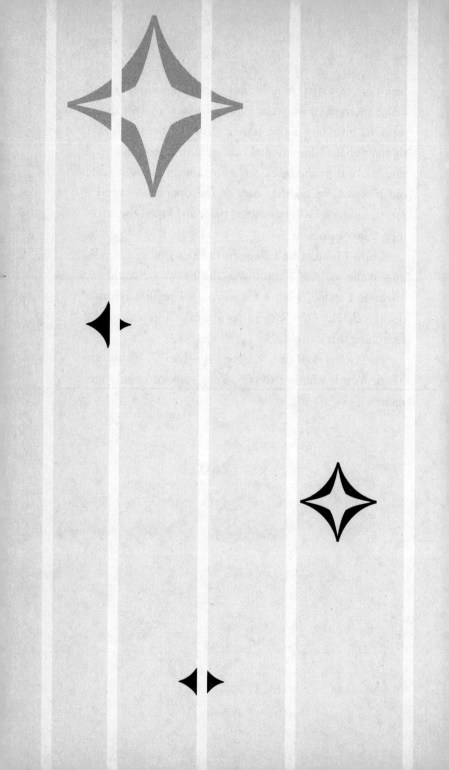

WE'RE A BRIDGE
OVER TROUBLED WATERS

Everyone in the office knew that Helen sometimes drank too much. A corporate lobbyist, she considered the liquid lunch part of her job. Occasionally some other member of the company had hinted that it was one thing to pour a politician's wine and pay for his lunch, but there was really no need to match the guest glass for glass. Two or three times a week, Helen entered the reception room, swayed for a minute or two, holding on to one of the double glass doors, and then aimed herself in the direction of her own office. Eventually, she reemerged, refreshed and ready to report.

Since Helen was good at getting people in power to see the benefit of whatever law or amendment she was proposing, management, if they minded at all, let the matter go. Then, when Helen turned sixty, they called her in, said that they felt she had become an alcoholic, and fired her.

Not only was this bad news for Helen, it was bad news for the rest of the office. Helen had acted this way for years;

her behavior hadn't changed. Rumors quickly spread that Helen had been fired so the company could avoid paying her retirement benefits. Office morale dropped.

Contrast this with the behavior of Stuart, who owns a large automobile-dealership in Texas. One of Stuart's salesmen, a man named Vincent, has a terrible temper. It first showed itself as occasional explosions aimed at the finance department. Vince would rage at them, accusing the department of delaying approval on his customers. Later, it spread to outbursts against other salesmen. Rustlers, he called them, insisting they were making off with his sales.

At this point Stuart called Vincent into his office and told him he needed help, a course in anger management; the company would pay. Vincent reluctantly agreed. "We ask for our employees' loyalty," Stuart told Alexandra. "In return, we try to support them. To my way of thinking, we're a bridge over troubled waters. We see people every day and can spot things that others might miss, like the way Vince was reacting to stress."

An outsider looking at the two incidents might say that the larger corporation didn't have the ability to deal with personal problems, but that's not true. Many companies make sure that supervisors keep an eye out for employees experiencing emotional problems and find ways to deal with them before they become a major irritant in the company. It's not the difference between large and small, but how a company views its relations with its employees. A wise manager knows how long it takes to train a replacement effectively, and how much time can be lost when employees begin to gossip about corporate goings-on. Employee loyalty is a company asset, even if it isn't entered on the books. Stuart knew this. "I made sure that the word slipped out that I'd reprimanded Vince and ordered him to get help. I wanted the other employees to know that I was aware of the problems he was causing. I also wanted them to know that I was trying to deal with it in a humane way. It makes people more secure when they know they work for a company that will try to help them with their problems. I had another objective in letting people know. If Vince didn't follow through, if he continued to let his anger rule him, no one would have thought it unfair to fire him. Those are my Magic Words—'We're a Bridge over Troubled Waters'—because they're kind and because they're smart."

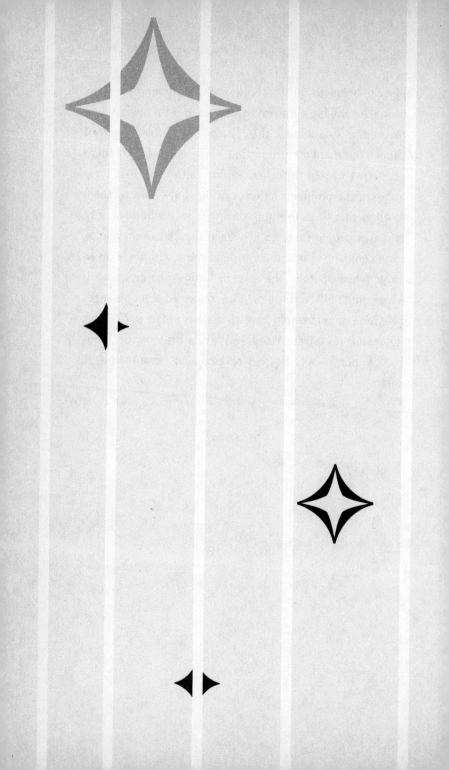

Howard had been working at his first job in publishing for about a year when he was told that he could go on a business trip to California. He was in the subsidiary-rights department at the time, and though he mainly sold paperback and book-club rights, he was also responsible for handling film rights. During his year at the company, he had put together a network of independent producers, and this trip was his chance to establish closer relationships with them. He had booked six to eight meetings a day, starting with breakfast and ending with dinner, and he was excited by the prospect of visiting all the film studios and meeting people he had only known on the phone.

When he boarded his flight to L.A., he was surprised to see that the head of the company, Geoff, was on the same plane. Of course, Geoff was seated in first class. So Howard was even more surprised when, a few minutes later, Geoff sat down next to him.

"I hope, Howard, you don't mind my taking this seat?"

"Of course not. But I thought you were seated in first class."

"I was."

"I don't understand."

"I have a simple rule that I always follow: 'We're All in the Same Class.' I will never fly in first class when a colleague is seated in coach. And, by the way, I do prefer sitting up front. I tried to get you a seat there, but wasn't able to. So, here I am."

Geoff went on to tell Howard that when he was starting out he worked for a man who always sat up front, while Geoff himself sat in the back. The boss took a limo to the airport, while Geoff, who lived in the same neighborhood, had to follow along in a taxi. He remembered how it made him feel, and he vowed never to do it to anyone who worked for him.

Howard never forgot Geoff's words. Several years later, a friend of Howard's came back from ten days in the Caribbean and mentioned that a large corporation had scheduled a meeting at the same resort. "The CEO was an arrogant kind of guy," said Howard's friend. "Can you believe that every night he had his top executives and their wives all eating at one long table, while he and his wife sat apart, with their own table and their own terribly expensive wines? What do you make of a guy like that?"

Howard knew exactly what to make of a guy like that, and he advised his friend and everyone else he knew who held the company's stock to sell. "Never put your money on a CEO who separates himself from the people who advise him," Howard said—rightly, it turned out, because eighteen months later that stock was lying flat on the ground.

Howard still remembers the thrill he felt when his CEO referred to him as a colleague and settled down next to him in a cramped airplane seat. That early experience convinced him that people who don't believe we're all in the same class don't make good managers. "How can you lead," he asks, "if you haven't any idea who's following?"

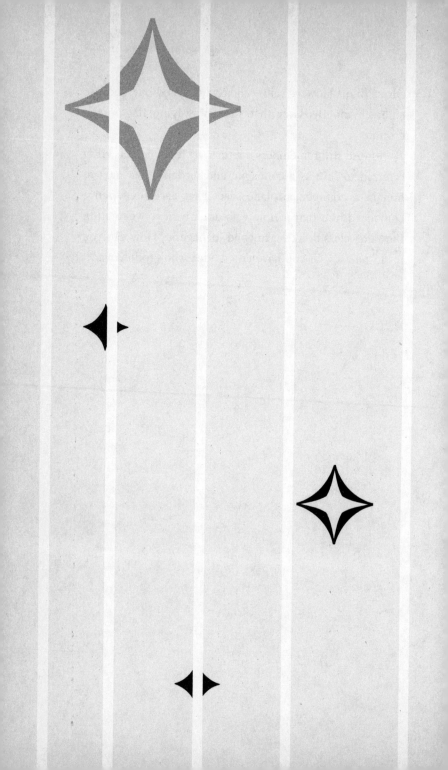

HANDS ON

In many companies the hands-on managing style has gone out of fashion, and rightly so, since it too often amounted to interfering with competent employees who functioned better when left on their own. But the backlash has created a new problem: employers who are so careful not to interfere that they fail to give help with the work when it's needed.

When our friend Ken was made manager of a small division in a manufacturing firm that makes household appliances, he received some advice from his boss.

"Matt was an observant and soft-spoken man," said Ken. "If he saw you do something wrong, he never pounced on you. In fact, he wouldn't do a thing unless he saw you make the same mistake twice. One morning, about a month after I'd been promoted, Matt asked me into his office.

" 'How are things going?' he asked.

"I said that things were pretty good, that I was still learning the production schedules and the systems but I was beginning to feel in control.

" 'What about the people?' Matt asked.

" 'The people?' I repeated. I wasn't sure what he meant.

" 'Your staff. How are things going with them?'

"I said that things were pretty good and that the staff was a lot easier to manage than the technical data I had to absorb."

Then Matt said that he'd noticed at last week's production meeting that Ken's assistant seemed to be having a difficult time handling the specs on our new line. Ken confessed that he hadn't noticed it, but said he'd only recently given her the assignment and that she'd pick it up in no time.

" 'I know she's smart,' Matt said. 'But I think she could use some help. You have to watch for things like that, Ken. A manager has to do a lot more than manage schedules and equipment. He also has to manage people. Making sure your staff is in control is one of the most important parts of your job.'

"I'd seen myself as the division quarterback," Ken said. "I'd call the plays, and the members of my team would execute them. Matt was telling me I was also the coach. There is a time when the people working for you need help. Often they're afraid to ask. A good manager knows when to keep hands off and when someone would appreciate a little hands-on."

Not long after Ken gave us his Magic Words, we heard a similar story from Barry, who lives in Detroit and owns a large construction company. Barry was telling us how close he came to having a serious problem because one of his project managers was used to playing "hands off."

"We needed to send a structural engineer to a site in Seattle where a building's foundation had begun to crack, and we needed someone to go immediately," said Barry. "The project manager said that he'd send Jay. I hesitated. Jay was perfect for the job, but his wife was expecting their first child, and the baby was due any day. No way Jay was going to agree to go. The project manager said, okay, he'd send Irwin. He got up to leave, but I stopped him. Did he really think Irwin was up to the job? He shrugged his shoulders. 'Who else is there?' I told him that since Irwin didn't have Jay's experience maybe we should try to use them both. I suggested that Irwin fly to Seattle and give us on-site readings and photographs via the Internet. With Irwin supplying the information and consulting with Jay, we'd have a better chance at getting the problem fixed. Irwin, who has great respect for Jay, agreed to the proposal. I think he was relieved to have the help. The problem was taken care of, and Irwin gained experience."

And we learned that "Hands On" can be just as important a management tool as "hands off."

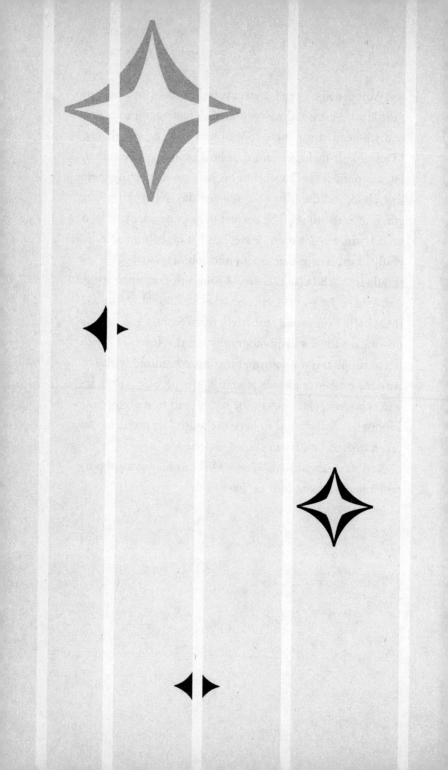

BENCH STRENGTH

Howard came up with these words shortly after he was given the opportunity, at the age of thirty-one, to head up a publishing company. They're derived partly from a quote that he came across at that time from Elbert Hubbard (1856–1915), an American businessman, who wrote, "There is something rarer than ability. It is the ability to recognize ability."

When Howard took over the company, it was at the bottom of the mass-market paperback business. Revenues were low and profits nonexistent. He felt that was why they had given him the opportunity: how much more could he screw the place up? In fact, in his first year the losses matched the revenues! The staff was not strong. There were few people of obvious ability and he realized quickly that he needed to hire, and hire fast. He required help in almost all areas: marketing, editorial, production, design— you name it. A year after making his key hires, he realized that he was only halfway there. The key people were in place, but there was no strong support staff, or, as they say in baseball, a bench. As on a baseball team, you need reserves in business. Things can't stop when someone's sick, or on holiday, or traveling, or on maternity leave. You need people who can step in and shoulder the burden.

He quickly found out that hiring skilled second, third, and fourth people in departments wasn't that easy. Why? "Well, truth be told," he says, "some of my new department heads didn't want strong people under them. I had a particular problem with Ted, my new marketing VP." The first three people whom Ted recommended had neither the experience nor the toughness for the job. Finally, Howard asked Ted to meet him for a drink after work.

" 'Ted,' Howard asked. 'How are things going?'

" 'Fine,' he said. 'I hope you like what I've been doing.' "

Howard told him that he was pleased with the way Ted had turned things around, but said he was concerned that Ted was working too hard and told him he definitely needed to have good backup.

Then Howard told him that he'd seen the candidates Ted had suggested for the job, and that he didn't think they were strong enough. "They'll need too much direction," Howard said, "and that's not going to cut your workload. We've got to find someone who's almost as good as you are."

"When I said that, Ted looked uncomfortable. He muttered something about how that was the kind of person he was looking for, but his edginess made me see right away what the problem was. Ted didn't *want* someone who was as good as he was. It made him nervous about his job."

Howard let it go for the time being because he wasn't

sure how to handle it. Finally, he called Ted and asked him to come to his office. It was baseball season, and Howard asked Ted if he had a favorite team. Surprise, it was the Yankees. So Howard said, "What if the pitcher hurts his arm? Have they hired weak backup so the pitcher won't get nervous about his job?" Ted replied, "Of course not." So Howard talked about bench strength and how the team isn't going to win if they have strong first-string players but no one to send in when someone is injured. He also told Ted that, as long as he was in charge, any underling who tried to get ahead by backstabbing a superior would be shown the door. Ted had left Howard's office and started down the hall when Howard called after him, "BENCH STRENGTH!"

"Two weeks later, I had it," said Howard.

Howard's experience revealed one reason why some companies are unable to fill positions with good people. Ginny, a friend of Alexandra's, gave her insight into another. Ginny worked for a small foundation dedicated to the environment, which was funded and run by an extremely rich man. The foundation had no problem hiring good scientists or good public-relations people, areas where the foundation's head, Timothy, had some experience. But the foundation had gone through three terrible treasurers in as many years. "You'd assume that because Timothy is rich he knows about money. But he doesn't," Ginny explained. "Someone else has always handled it for him. A person Tim is interviewing for the job of treasurer can talk gobbledygook, and even though Timothy is very smart, he assumes that because he doesn't understand it, it must be brilliant." Ginny and the other staff members finally ganged up on their boss. They, too, had figured out that it takes ability to recognize ability. The foundation had bench strength when it came to promoting their cause or giving money to good people; it had none at all when it came to accounting for the money they had. In the future, Timothy has promised to let the brokerage firm that handles his own finances hire a treasurer for the foundation. Sometimes the only way to get bench strength is to ask advice from someone outside.

IT STARTS WITH
ONE SET OF LIPS

Sam, the vice-president of a small pharmaceutical company, says he first noticed that his company had a problem when he walked past the watercooler. "A woman named Marge from our accounting office was holding forth. When she saw me, she suddenly stopped talking and hurried off."

Sam might not have paid any attention to the incident, but shortly afterward he began to hear rumors that he was in the middle of negotiating a merger with another company. He told the few people who were bold enough to ask that the rumors were untrue. His denials had no effect. Sam, trying to figure out how the rumor had gotten started, remembered that a few months ago he had asked Marge to gather figures for him on the performance of one of their rivals. Marge must have drawn her own conclusions as to why he wanted the financial information, and, after jumping to a wrong conclusion, spread it through the office.

Sam didn't like it, but he decided there wasn't much he could do. Until the following week, when his assistant informed him that the entire office was speculating about the merger, wondering if their jobs would be eliminated. Key employees were discussing whether it would be wise to move on.

During the war the government had a slogan, "Loose Lips Sink Ships"; they can damage companies, too. Not every office has a dangerous gossip—the kind of person who learns to read important documents upside down to become privy to inside information—but even one on the payroll can cause company chaos.

Employees who spread rumors all seem to have two things in common:

They have an insatiable desire to find out what's going on.

When they pass it on (which they do as quickly as they can), they put a spin on the information that's sure to disrupt the usual routine of the office.

Talk that spreads outside the office can play havoc with a company's stock, but even talk within the company hurts productivity. People who should be concentrating on their own work are at a colleague's desk, speculating on things to come. Sam said that, faced with the wildfire he suspected Marge of starting, "I actually thought about calling her in and explaining the damage she was doing. But you can never call back a rumor. And I couldn't prove she was the source. It was a suspicion, not a fact. If she was the culprit, my confronting her would make it worse: my meeting with her would go on the grapevine as well. So I called the staff together, said that there were no negotiations for a merger, that the rumor may have been based on my wanting to check another company's performance figures, and that I would be grateful if they would shut up. I didn't actually say that, but I made it clear that the gossip wasn't doing the company any good.

"Eventually, the rumor died of starvation: nothing happened to feed it, and people just let it go. Everything got back to normal. With one small change. I can't be absolutely sure that Marge was the source of the rumor, but now when I want something from the accounting department I ask someone else to get it for me. And I try to keep an eye on who's holding forth at the watercooler. Trouble in an office starts with one set of lips. You can't stop a rumor once it gets started, but you can do your best to stop it before it begins."

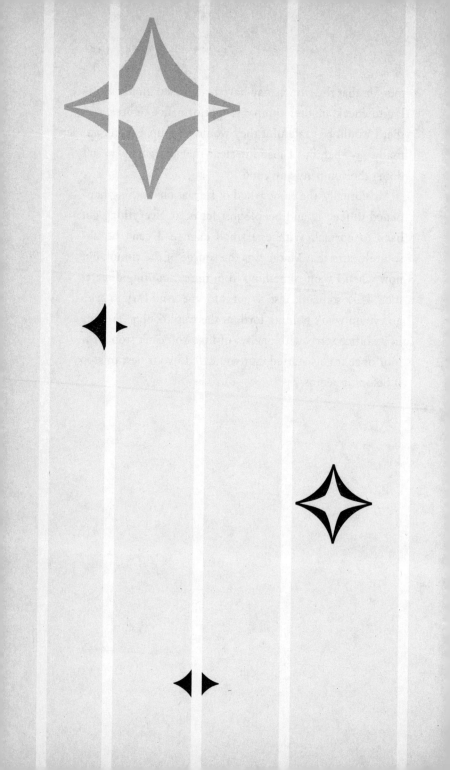

You don't have to move very far up in the ranks of management before you'll have to do something you hate. You'll have to fire someone.

"The first time, I made a mess of it," said Martin, a mid-level manager in a large corporation that has gone through two downsizings in the last ten years. "Mercifully, time has dimmed the memory, but I think that I actually told the guy that it was as hard on me as it was on him."

Naturally, Martin recalls, the man did not agree. He argued to save his job. "He said he wanted a chance to put together a memo that explained why his position was important and shouldn't be eliminated."

Martin looks embarrassed as he admits, "I let him. I knew the decision was made and it wasn't going to be changed, but I convinced myself that he'd feel better if he had a chance to fight."

Martin acknowledges that, by backing off, he simply prolonged the agony. The time the man spent putting together a defense would have been better spent putting together a résumé. "The job was gone; I should have been helping him find another, or at least made it clear that he should start looking. But I let him waste his time," says Martin. "I thought I was being kind, making him feel better, but when I look back, I realize I did it to make myself feel better. I didn't want to be the bad guy, the messenger arriving with terrible news."

Now, says Martin, his motto is "Ready, Aim, Fire."

"Quicker is kinder," he insists, and asks, "Why do people think it's better to string someone along? If it's going to happen, get it over with." He explains that he's got firing down to a formula. "If someone is worth keeping, I argue with the higher-ups before the decision is made. If the job is still eliminated, I try to find that person another job within the company. If that fails, I tell the employee he's performed well, that losing the job is not his fault, and I do what I can to help him find a place somewhere else. I always try to help the person figure out what his next move should be. I tell him that I'll make whatever calls are necessary to find out what jobs might be open and even put in a good word for him. It's the least I can do.

"When someone is being let go because he's not up to the job, I'm honest about it. Kind, but honest. If I don't tell someone what he's doing wrong, why he's being let go, how is he ever going to do a job where he gets it right?"

Unfortunately, both of us have had to fire people, and we would agree with everything Martin says and add a few things of our own.

Howard insists that, no matter how difficult, the only way to fire a person is face to face.

"I once had to fire an employee (one that I liked a lot, by the way) who worked in our Los Angeles office. I flew early in the morning to L.A., told him the bad news over lunch, and then took the red-eye back. It was a long, exhausting day, but it was the only way I could do it. You should *never, never* terminate an employee by telephone, or letter, or e-mail, and you certainly shouldn't let him or her get the news via office smoke signals. He deserves to be told straight on, in your office. And make sure you tell your assistant to hold your calls. A lot of times the person you're letting go hasn't done anything wrong. Budgets get cut, staffs are reduced, and you find yourself sending good people out onto the street. And one other thing: sometimes you're firing someone because he's screwed up, or because he's a troublemaker. Always check with the legal department on what you should say and what you shouldn't. You don't want to give a dissatisfied employee a chance to sue."

Alexandra also insists on dealing with the person one on one. "Every person deserves that. I also prepare myself to answer any questions they may have regarding severance, health benefits, vacation pay, you name it. If at all possible, I let them have a hand in how the press release—if there is to be one—will be worded. And I prepare myself to listen. No matter how long it takes, I'm there for the person and I'll try to help in any way I can."

These Magic Words mean a lot to us because we've been on both sides of the desk. Yup, we've both been canned. In fact, we believe that no one should be allowed to fire someone who hasn't been through the experience himself.

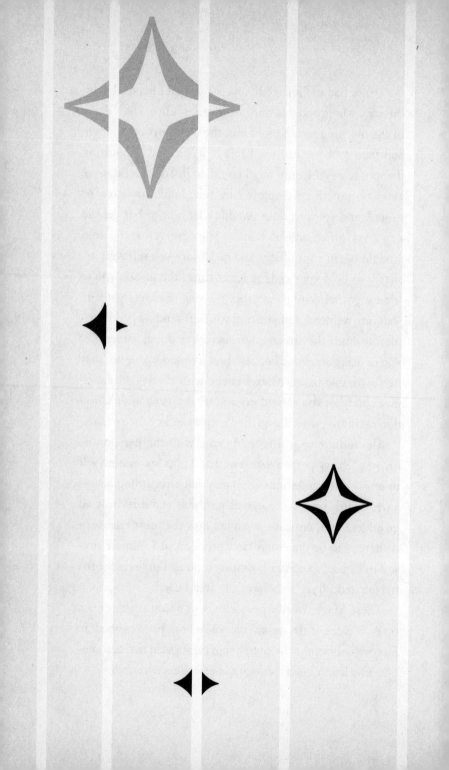

ABOVE ME IS
NO-MAN'S-LAND

An end run is a good thing in football, because everyone on the team has the same goal—squashing the opposition. But in an office, in theory at least, there is no opposition. Everyone is a member of the same team, even that disgruntled employee who feels that the lead horse is trotting off in the wrong direction.

Rob learned the damage that can be done by a dissatisfied staff member when he took his first management job, with a Western telephone company. In promoting an employee to replace a man who'd recently retired, he made an enemy of the man he'd passed over. At first the enmity came out indirectly—reports completed a day late, or critical comments posed as innocent questions: "Have you taken into account the repercussions of cutting the costs of local calls?"

Gradually, the man's opposition became more overt and he openly questioned Rob's decisions. On the day Rob announced a plan to install more public phones in the poorer sections of the city, the employee took his dissent to the top.

The president, who had helped formulate the plan, knew as well as Rob did that the increased number of public phones wasn't philanthropy. It was a response to pressure from a citizens' group. The employee's end run did him no good, but it didn't help Rob, either. The president told Rob to keep his departmental squabbles to himself, not to let them bother the boss.

That's when Rob made his organizational chart. It was a little like a medieval map, where the edges of the known world were marked by the legend "Beyond This There Be Dragons." Rob wanted his staff to know that above him there were dragons. Over his name there were large letters: "No-Man's-Land."

From that time on, whenever Rob hired a new staff member, he brought out the chart and made it clear that those who ventured over his head risked their own.

Rob's lecture about no-man's-land isn't based on ego. He wants his department to run smoothly, and he knows that members of his staff may not be aware of all the factors involved in a decision. Rob also knows that, to ensure that no one goes over his head, he has to encourage his employees to bring their grievances and differences directly to him. "You can tell your staff not to end-run you as often as you want," says Rob, "but if you don't listen to their complaints and problems, someone is going to take them upstairs."

WHEN THE WATER'S RISING, HEAD FOR THE TOP

"Above Me is No-Man's-Land," Rob warned his employees, and he was right. Problems should be solved where they originate, and Rob's open-door policy made sure that they were. But not all managers are good ones, and not all rules are ironclad. Having given you the preceding Magic Words, we now offer you some that tell you when to break the rule.

Mary Beth had once worked for Alexandra, but different jobs had taken them in different directions. When they ran into each other at a luncheon, they spent the time catching up. Mary Beth told Alexandra about her new job, handling communications and public relations for a corporation whose president was distinctly scandal-prone, and Alexandra told Mary Beth about her own project—compiling Magic Words that would help people cope with difficult business situations.

"I've got some great ones," Mary Beth volunteered. "Actually, they're my husband's, but if Charlie hadn't come up with them, we might be sitting on our sofas out on the sidewalk, evicted for failing to pay our mortgage. With three children in private school, we don't have much margin."

Naturally, Alexandra wanted to know what had happened, and Mary Beth suggested that she call Charlie. Alexandra did, and learned Charlie's story and the Magic Words that saved his job.

"I was one of the company's golden boys until the vice-president who oversaw my division quit and was replaced by a new man. At first I couldn't decide whether he didn't like me or whether he was just incompetent. I know now it was the latter, but he changed everything I did. Every report was rewritten. Every suggestion I made was altered. People I relied on were transferred out of my division. Within three months, everything was a mess. I asked for a meeting and told him I thought what he was doing was hurting my division. He said I was too parochial. I couldn't see the 'big picture.'

"At six months, I got a notice from on high, warning me that if I couldn't get my division back on track I'd better start looking for another job. I was knee-deep in the big muddy, and I decided it was time to climb out. All I could think about was drowning, and I thought, What does common sense tell us? When the water's rising, head for the top. I went to the president with my original reports and suggestions, statistics on what my division had produced before the change and after. Maybe it wouldn't have worked if I'd been the only one, but the vice-president had messed up other areas as well. The president listened to me, and not long after, Mr. Mess Up was out."

Charlie's story reminded Alexandra of another one, which didn't end so well. She had a friend who had worked for a magazine on the West Coast. When a new articles editor took over, Alexandra's friend found all his story ideas rejected. When he wrote on the subjects the new editor assigned, his copy was changed, entire sections crucial to understanding the story cut out. Alexandra's friend didn't go to the editor in chief. He decided instead to ride it out and not make trouble, convinced that the new editor was so bad he'd be out on his ear before long.

After six months, it was the writer who was out on his ear. The reason: his work had fallen off badly, and his stories no longer made sense. When a work situation has deteriorated to the point where it threatens your job, break the rules.

Charlie says that his friends warned him, "You're taking a big chance. You could get fired." But, says Charlie, "if I hadn't gone to the top, the water would have risen right over my head. I would have drowned anyway."

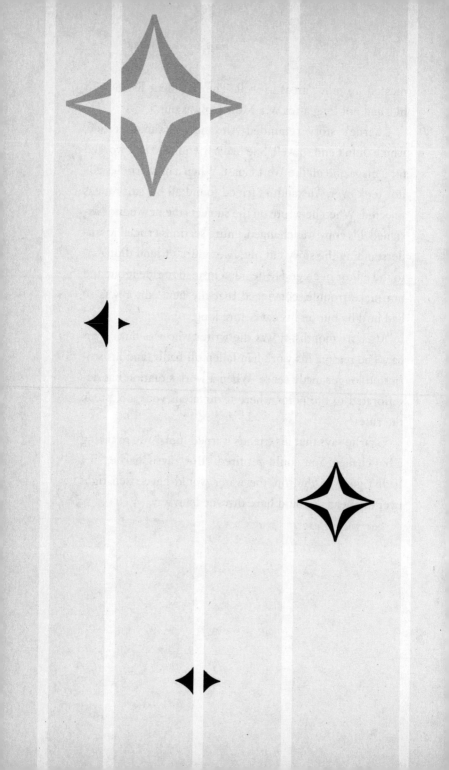

A FOUR-LEGGED TABLE
CAN'T STAND ON THREE LEGS

These Magic Words come from Reed, a sales executive for a French firm that makes medical-waste disposal systems. His job takes him all over the northeastern United States and, naturally, to France, where he frequently convoys small groups of potential customers so they can see that the waste has been rendered into the small particles the government requires. During his first three years, Reed told Alexandra, he was his company's top performer. "I was pretty impressed with myself back then," he says. "I was convinced I could sell anyone anything."

The next time Reed herded a group to France, they watched a very different demonstration. "I had arranged everyone in a circle so they'd each be able to see what was going on. I gave a little pep talk about the company, and then I raised my arm—one finger pointing at the sky, very dramatic, you know—and announced, 'And now you'll see what we can do.' I lowered my arm so that my finger was pointing at the machine. That was the cue for the operator to start it up. Which he did. Well, instead of the machine going into action, there was a coughing and sputtering noise. The damn thing wasn't working.

"I'd spent an enormous amount of time looking into ways in which our product could help these people; I'd convinced them it was something they should buy; I'd brought them all the way to France—and in two hours at the plant, all my work was wiped out. Why should they believe me when I told them the system was reliable? We'd just demonstrated that it wasn't. I'm a good salesman, but that experience taught me a lesson. None of us stand alone."

Reed had learned that one of the most important parts of the business world is often invisible. It's the backroom divisions. Reed's company lost a sale because it failed to focus on the need for an efficient service department. They had fallen into a pattern all too familiar in big companies today: spend the money on advertising or sales to attract new customers; forget about carefully and consistently monitoring the product or providing support to existing customers.

Successful managers see their company as a series of interlocking parts. Each division is important on its own, but it's also necessary to the support of the others. That's the only way to be sure that the product is as good as the advertising.

"I guess I thought it was new sales that kept the company going," says Reed, "but that fiasco really taught me about service. I learned to keep in close touch with the people who make things work. When we got a new head for the service department, I sent him a gift and a note telling him how much I needed his support. I wrote, 'A four-legged table can't stand on three legs. Knock off one and the table falls down.' "

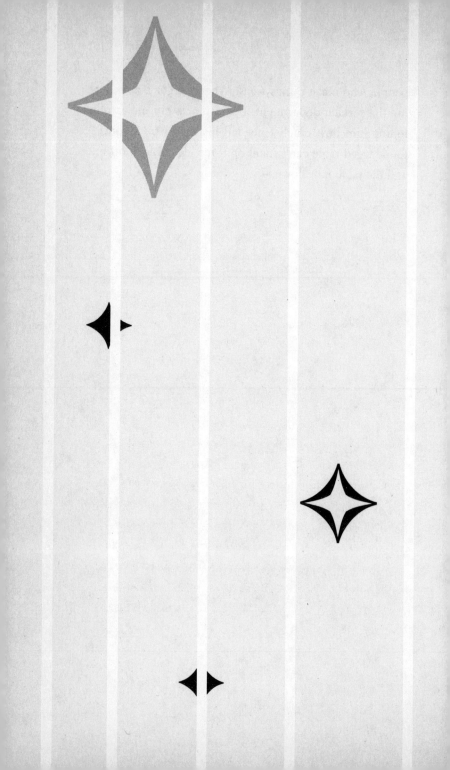

Morton gave us these Magic Words, and he told us what they meant. They are not a ban on the secret noontime rendezvous that keeps an affair secret from a suspicious spouse, Morton says; they mean that, when he hires, he doesn't hire a man or a woman, he hires the person who's right for the job. "I tell them there's no sex in this office. And since there's no sex, naturally I never expect to see sexual harassment."

It sounds so simple, and for Morton, director of personnel at a large computer company, it is. Dirty jokes or comments to a woman, exclusion of a woman salesperson from the men's Friday-afternoon golf game, even the exclusion of men from a secretary's baby shower all have sent Morton to the computer keyboard to fire off one of his now famous memos: "LET ME REMIND YOU. THERE IS NO SEX IN THIS OFFICE."

Morton is hypersensitive to potential charges of sexual harassment, and when he saw the head of accounting standing too close to one of his staff, he feared his memos weren't doing the trick. Morton convened a seminar on keeping sex out of the office. *All* staff members, no matter how high their position, were required to attend what Morton called a session on hands-off management.

There was a lawyer specializing in cases of sexual harassment, a psychologist, and an acting teacher who described how we reveal ourselves through body language. Morton was pleased to see that one of her examples, acted out by two staff members, involved a manager standing close to and touching a female staff member. What the expert had to say was no surprise to the women on the staff. "Men and women read things differently," she said, mentioning studies in which men have said they'd be more flattered than offended if someone "came on" to them in the office. Men, more often in a position of power, aren't made to feel that their job depends on being nice to the boss.

None of this is news, but before we ran into Morton we had been trying to think of Magic Words women could use to fend off unwelcome attentions. Each of us came up with a few snappy put-downs for those times when sex interferes with a career. We reluctantly decided that the only woman we could imagine saying them was the late Marlene Dietrich, and even she wouldn't be able to pull them off without a feather boa.

So this is what we learned. Sexual harassment isn't something women can deal with by themselves. Ridding an office of the atmosphere that allows it to exist doesn't fall into the realm of Managing Yourself, or Managing

Shoulder to Shoulder. It's nice to envision women marching arm in arm on the CEO's office, but when they got
there, they'd probably feel like fools. And wonder if, somewhere in the background, someone was writing down their
names.

Ridding the office of sexual inequality is the job of
those Managing Down, who need to use whatever means
it takes to create a company where Morton's Magic Words
hold sway: "No Sex in the Office."

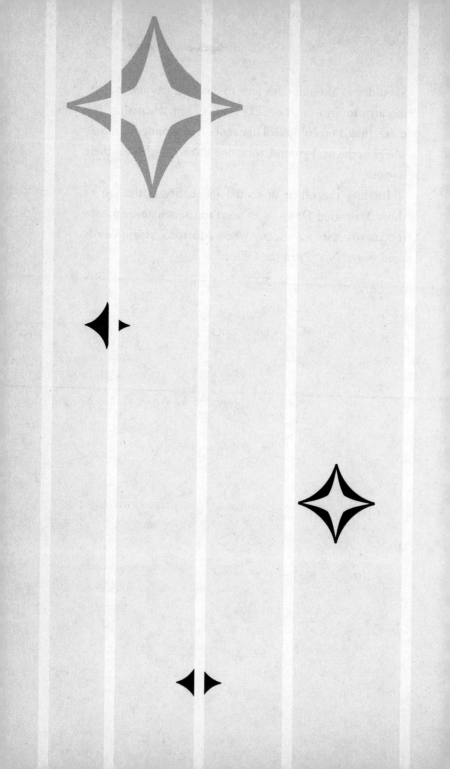

This is what Harry says, and when he does he gets a twinkle in his eye and you get the feeling that he wishes he hadn't recently retired after twenty years of running a large toy company. Sounds like fun, doesn't it, running a toy company? But Harry, a large, bearlike man with a ready smile, always said that latching on to the toy that would have mothers marching up the aisle was "as easy as brokering a peace settlement in the Middle East." We loved hearing his stories about the toy business and the chances he took. You would have heard of the famous doll that made Christmas a misery for those parents who couldn't buy it. But no one remembers the little suitcase based on the game My Grandmother's Trunk, because it never got out of the warehouse. The catch was defective, and when children picked up the suitcase, all ready to trot off and visit Granny, it spewed its contents out onto the floor.

Harry, more than most businesspeople we know, has had an up-and-down career.

"When I think back," he told us recently, "it's a little like mountain climbing. Quite a few positive spikes, but probably a few more steep and scary drops. I realized quite a while ago that I wouldn't be around for long in this business if I didn't really enjoy myself during the fat times. And, more important, if I learned not to let the bad times do me in."

One of the things that put Harry into the bad times was the Magneto Family. "The orders just flooded in. Toys 'R' Us, F.A.O., everybody was screaming to have more. We produced it in Taipei, and the factory couldn't keep up. I was frantic. I had to find another supplier fast. I was going to give the work to a company in the Philippines, but they were expensive. I knew they'd get it out on time, but I was reluctant to cut into my profits. Now, I have to admit that my margin on this toy was terrific, but the year before had been a tough one. I wanted to make every last dollar I could. So I gave the order to a factory in Indonesia, one I'd never done any business with. Why? Their prices were sensational. I'm sure you know the end of this story.

"Not only was their delivery late, but more than half the toys they produced for us were unacceptable. I learned the hard way that sometimes saving a few cents means losing a lot of dollars. But over the years, I've figured out that it's the bad times that make you learn. And I'll tell you something else. It's the bad times that made our company a family. We all pulled together, and we always came through. It wasn't like so many companies today. When we had lean years, we all tightened our belts. And when we hit it, everyone got a share. I read now about these companies where the big guys take it all and the little guys get nothing. That's no way to run a business. Not if you want it to last. Loyalty is something you have to build. It's everybody pulling together that makes the bad times not so bad.

"You know where I got my Magic Words? The night watchman. It was a year when we were getting trounced. I thought I'd gotten the best lineup I'd ever had, and guess what took over the market? Ninja Turtles! I was in the warehouse late one night, and the watchman, a guy who'd been around for years, shuffles over. 'Bad times ain't so bad, Harry. They're the step right below good times. I've been thinking about how next year we can be number one. We can do samurai snails. Turtles aren't the only ones that already got their armor.' To this day I don't know if he was being funny, but I wouldn't trade that conversation for Harry Potter's broomstick.

"If you have a company and you run it right, everyone cares what happens. And when you see how hard your employees work, how much energy they give to make things succeed, you realize that even the bad times ain't that bad."

© MARA BODIS-WOLLNER

About the Authors

HOWARD KAMINSKY was the president and publisher of three major publishing houses: Warner Books, Random House, and William Morrow/Avon. Also the author of several screenplays, five novels (co-written with his wife, Susan), and numerous magazine articles, he lives in New York City and Connecticut.

ALEXANDRA PENNEY's four bestsellers include the megahit *How to Make Love to a Man*. In addition to serving as editor in chief of *Self* magazine, she has written lifestyle columns for the *New York Times Magazine* and contributed regularly to numerous other publications. She lives in New York City.